Cross-cultural Organizational and Financial Training

Praise for this book

'In any society, culture and money have complicated relationships, norm and standards. The practical and elegant way in which John Cammack connects the two when building human and organisational capacity is a testament to both his wide experience and contextual sensitivity. Readers will gain more than they might expect from spending time absorbing and applying what these pages have to offer.'
Professor Alan Fowler, the Wits Business School,
and co-founder of INTRAC

'John Cammack's timely guide on cross cultural training provides a thorough walk-through of how to organize and deliver a participation-driven workshop or training module anywhere in the world. Professor Cammack's impressive teaching experience across three continents renders his work invaluable to those seeking to benefit from grassroots knowledge and how international financial frameworks may be best interpreted to serve local communities.'
Dr Susan H. Perry, The American University of Paris

Cross-cultural Organizational and Financial Training
A practical guide

John Cammack

Practical Action Publishing Ltd
27a, Albert Street, Rugby, Warwickshire, CV21 2SG, UK

www.practicalactionpublishing.com

© John Cammack, 2020

The moral right of the editors to be identified as editors of the work and the contributors to be identified as contributors of this work have been asserted under sections 77 and 78 of the Copyright Design and Patents Act 1988.

All rights reserved. No part of this publication may be reprinted or reproduced or utilized in any form or by any electronic, mechanical, or other means, now known or hereafter invented, including photocopying and recording, or in any information storage or retrieval system, without the written permission of the publishers.

Product or corporate names may be trademarks or registered trademarks, and are used only for identification and explanation without intent to infringe.

A catalogue record for this book is available from the British Library.

A catalogue record for this book has been requested from the Library of Congress.

978-1-788531-054 Paperback
978-1-788531-061 Hardback
978-1-788531-078 Epub
978-1-788531-085 PDF

Citation: Cammack, J. (2020) *Cross-cultural Organizational and Financial Training: A practical guide*, Rugby, UK: Practical Action Publishing <http://dx.doi.org/10.3362/9781788531085>.

Since 1974, Practical Action Publishing has published and disseminated books and information in support of international development work throughout the world. Practical Action Publishing is a trading name of Practical Action Publishing Ltd (Company Reg. No. 1159018), the wholly owned publishing company of Practical Action. Practical Action Publishing trades only in support of its parent charity objectives and any profits are covenanted back to Practical Action (Charity Reg. No. 247257, Group VAT Registration No. 880 9924 76).

The views and opinions in this publication are those of the author and do not represent those of Practical Action Publishing Ltd or its parent charity Practical Action. Reasonable efforts have been made to publish reliable data and information, but the authors and publisher cannot assume responsibility for the validity of all materials or for the consequences of their use.

Cover illustration by Graham-Cameron Illustration

Contents

Preface	ix
Acknowledgements	xi
Boxes, figures, and tables	xiii
Glossary	xv
About the author	xix

1. The challenges of cross-cultural training and how to respond — **1**
    Challenges for the trainer — 1
    Challenges for the participant — 4

2. Understanding other cultures — **9**
    Identifying differences in cultures — 9
    International cultures: 'high-context' and 'low-context' — 10
    International cultures: seven dimensions of culture — 14
    Saving face — 19
    Do and don'ts in other cultures — 20
    More thoughts about culture — 21

3. Making your training work — **23**
    Training or facilitation? — 23
    Participatory training style — 24
    Before the training starts — 26
    Designing and preparing the content — 36
    Delivering the training — 42
    Monitoring, evaluation, and learning after the training — 54
    More thoughts on training — 60

4 Practical techniques for training cross-culturally — **61**
    Welcoming: helping participants feel comfortable — 61

Content	65
Practical arrangements	68

5 Planning and delivering cross-cultural online training — 71

Advantages and disadvantages of online training	72
Types of online training	72
Getting the practicalities right	74
Cross-cultural training online	80
Before the training starts	84
Designing and preparing the content	85
Delivering the training	85
Monitoring, evaluation, and learning after the training	89

6 Cross-cultural financial training — 91

Specific challenges with finance training	91
Responding to these challenges	92
International document names, financial terms and numbering systems	98
Tips when delivering finance training	101

7 Training in specific countries — 103

Training in Bangladesh	104
Training in Cambodia	108
Training in Ethiopia	113
Training in Ghana	119
Training in India	123
Training in Jordan	129
Training in Kenya	133
Training in Pakistan	138
Training in United Kingdom	143
Training in Zambia	149
Summary of key points to remember when training and working cross-culturally	153
Travel practicalities	158

8 Examples of cross-cultural training — **161**
- Eye contact — 161
- Upsetting a participant — 162
- A trip out - 1 — 162
- A trip out - 2 — 162
- Being critical — 163
- Risk taking — 163
- Too much participation — 164
- Saving face — 164
- Is everything all right? — 165

9 Training cross-culturally: frequently asked questions — **167**
- Working with participants — 167
- Questions and answers — 175
- Learning objectives — 177
- Participatory training and learning — 177
- Group work — 178
- Online training — 180
- Timing — 183
- Feedback — 184

10 Introductory activities — **189**
- The 'horn' game — 189
- Remember one of your influential teachers — 190
- Memories — 191
- Picture it — 191
- Six — 192
- Hopes and concerns — 193
- Have a break — 194

11 Energizing activities — **195**
- Tableau — 195
- Terminology quiz — 196
- Just a minute — 197

Consolidating questions	197
Key learning poster	198
Fives and sevens	198
Writing in the air	199

12 Concluding activities 201

What learning are you taking away from this training?	201
Learning log	202
What next?	203
Postcards	203
One more question?	204
Storytelling	204
Presenting certificates	205
One word	206

Appendix 1: Self-assessment of high-context and low-context culture	207
What the rankings suggest and how to develop your cultural skills in training	208
Appendix 2: Action verbs for writing learning objectives	211
References and resources	213
End note	219
Index	221

Preface

This book is designed for new, and not so new, trainers who are working across cultural boundaries. There are many books giving guidance on training individuals and groups. However, there is a lack of material about how to train in an organizational setting when working with people from different cultural backgrounds. This can be even more challenging when using English with participants for whom it is their second or third language. However, cultural difference is more than just about language, and also includes differing values, attitudes, and behaviour. This can be between countries and regions, groups and individuals, and sectors and organizations.

This book assumes that you or your team are:

- *Offering face-to-face or online training within an organizational setting.* This might be simply working informally with one person trying to upgrade their skills, perhaps acting as a coach or mentor, or with a group in a more formal setting.
- *Responsible for offering training in the English language.* That the English language is the main means of communicating.
- *Providing one or more organizational topics.* For staff and other stakeholders.
- *Working across cultural boundaries.* For example, with people who are from different ethnic backgrounds, from other parts of the world, or who have a different professional or organizational culture from that of the trainer.

The book is primarily written for trainers in the international non-profit sector. However, it can be used by people training cross-culturally in government, commercial, and for-profit sectors, and in faith-based organizations. It can also be used by those teaching and learning in universities and colleges.

It considers the general challenges in training cross-culturally, how to best understand other cultures, and offers tools, techniques, and best practice. It also looks in-depth at cultural differences using 10 specific countries as examples. Many organizations in these countries regularly host training events that require cross-cultural skills. However, this focus aims to help trainers to consider similar issues, wherever training is held. Finally, the book provides a useful toolkit of activities.

The book is based on the author's experience of designing and delivering both face-to-face and online training in organizational and financial management, in many cultures and countries. It is also informed by research carried out with other experienced operational and training practitioners, including from the countries featured.

John Cammack
Oxford, United Kingdom

Acknowledgements

I am grateful to the many people who have had an input into this book. Thanks to the Practical Action Publishing team Chloe Callan-Foster, Rosanna Denning, Katarzyna Markowska, Clare Tawney, Andrea Johnson and Denise Hastings; and Martha Hardy for the cover illustration. Thanks, too, to those who have read through the earlier drafts, especially the country sections, and given practical suggestions for improvements. Also, to those who have given permission to reproduce or amend an item that they created.

Numerous people have shared their insights and contributed to this research about cross-cultural training, and in particular how this works in the 10 specific countries selected. These include: Frehiwot Alebachew (Hope International, Ethiopia), Tala Al Najjar (RedR, Jordan), Urvashi Asthana (Practical Action, India), Lourdes Baptista (Water Aid, India), Anne Borrowdale, Celia Boyd (SHE investments, Cambodia), Sokanta Chanda (GIZ Thailand), Charles Dollie, Hannah Dollie, Lara Farah (RedR, Jordan), Shadab Fariduddin (NGO Resource Centre, Pakistan), Nour Habjoka (RedR Jordan), Gabriel Helmy, Khizar Hyatt (Oxfam, Pakistan), Philippe Le Jalle, Hiwot Jemberu (Farm Africa, Ethiopia), Mick Kain, Habatamu Kitaba (Farm Africa, Ethiopia), Loret Loumouamou (Institute for the Healing of Memories, South Africa), John Lowrie, Achyut Luitel (Pactical Action, Nepal), Aragaw Hailu Mengesha (Life and Peace Institute, Ethiopia), Dennis Mulenga, Muriuki Muriungi, Alick Nyirenda (Norwegian Association of the Disabled, Zambia), Peter Ogolla, Gita Patel (Practical Action, UK), Dr Sanjay Patra (Financial Management Service Foundation, India), Dr Gaffar Peang-Meth, David Phillips, Raed Rajab, Dr Abdul Hadi Rashaq, Md. Maksudur Rahman (Water & Sanitation for the Urban Poor, Bangladesh), Gopal Rao, Riasat H. Rashtee (GIZ, Thailand), Md Mosleh Uddin Sadeque, Grace Samkange, Sambo Samrith (Centre for Conflict and Peace Studies, Cambodia), Rowshan Sharmin Jahan, Jeff Shum

(All Ears, Cambodia), P.K. Sriraman (Water Aid, India), Fatima Swartz (Institute for the Healing of Memories, South Africa), Zemenu Tadesse (Pestalozzi Children's Foundation, Ethiopia), Dr Feleke Tadele, Lay Pek Try (Cambodia Community Finance Network, Cambodia), Rosemary Tucker, Glyn Vaughan (All Ears, Cambodia), and Chrissie Webb. I am grateful to the Daughters of Wisdom, Romsey for providing me with a quiet space to write.

Thanks also to all those who have participated in training events, coaching sessions, and consultancy work with me over many years. They have helped my understanding of the great joy of finding out about other cultures, and practical ways of building bridges between them. Much of their wisdom is distilled throughout this book.

Last but not least, I thank Freda Cammack and Stephen Cammack for their constant and loyal support in the process of research and writing this book, and for giving me invaluable suggestions on the earlier versions of the text.

Boxes, figures, and tables

Boxes

1.1	A trainer's story	2
1.2	A participant's story	4
2.1	You lost me at 'hello'	10
3.1	What is the difference between a trainer and facilitator?	24
3.2	Example of a participatory approach to training	25
3.3	Example of a 'welcome message' for participants	33
3.4	Example of a training requirements format	35
3.5	Giving instructions when working across cultures	43
3.6	Dos and don'ts of presenting	49
3.7	Dos and don'ts when *asking* questions	53
3.8	Dos and don'ts when *answering* questions	54
3.9	Story: training and follow-up	59
5.1	Summary of advantages and disadvantages of cross-cultural online training	73
5.2	Example of a checklist for the trainer to start a 'live' event	88
6.1	Deciding whether to use a training event to build financial management capacity	93
7.1	Fact file: Bangladesh	105
7.2	Fact file: Cambodia	109
7.3	Fact file: Ethiopia	114
7.4	Fact file: Ghana	119
7.5	Fact file: India	124
7.6	Fact file: Jordan	129
7.7	Fact file: Kenya	133
7.8	Fact file: Pakistan	138
7.9	Fact file: United Kingdom	144
7.10	Fact file: Zambia	149

Figures

1.1	Possible responses to 'how do you prefer to learn?'	7
2.1	Seven dimensions of culture	15

3.1	Example of mind-mapping a training session	37
3.2	How to prioritize training content	39
3.3	Example of a welcome poster	45
3.4	Example of a 'road map'	47
4.1	Welcome, content, and practical approaches	62
5.1	Some tools for participatory online training	82
12.1	Shield	202

Tables

2.1	Aspects of high- and low-context cultures	11
3.1	Example of a training plan	40
5.1	Summary of online training and learning delivery options	75
6.1	Alternative names for financial documents used internationally	99
6.2	Alternative names for financial terms used internationally	99
6.3	Arabic and Western numbers	101
A.1	Self-assessment of high-context and low-context culture	207
A.2	Action verbs for writing learning objectives	211

Glossary

Activity Part of a training course designed to help learning

Big picture Overview of a topic

Brainstorming Working with a group to produce creative solutions with the freedom to suggest anything, no matter how unusual. Writing up ideas for all to see, without comment. Usually an evaluation follows, to identify the most workable ideas

Buzz sessions Breaking a large group into smaller 'buzz' groups to stimulate discussion and add variety to a training session

Closed question A question requiring a 'yes' or 'no' answer

Culture 'The values, attitudes, and behaviour in a given group of most of the people most of the time' (Munter, 1993)

Energizer An *activity* or game to boost a group's energy perhaps after a demanding session, or when there has been a lot of sitting and listening

Electronic-training and learning (or E- training) *See Online training*

Face-to-face training Where both the trainer(s) and participants are all in the same place

Facilitator Someone who works with a group to think through issues and assist participants in learning for themselves. This may involve discussion, looking at possible outcomes, and building consensus in the group. The facilitator must be independent and non-judgemental

Family name A name used in addition to a *given name* or *'known by' name*. Sometimes a name that members of a family share, or sometimes the name of a parent added to the *given name*

Finance people Those who work with financial information and systems for most of their time

Flip chart A pad of A1 sized paper displayed on a stand for presentations. It can be turned over to show a new page. Sometimes called a 'flip over chart'

Forum A online system where participants can send, read, or reply to messages about a particular topic. Also know as Online Forum

Given name The name chosen by parents at birth by which an individual is known. See also *'known by' name*

GMT Greenwich Mean Time. The standard measure of time by which all time zones are measured. Also called 'universal coordinated time', UTC

Ground rules Rules, agreed by participants and trainers, for their expected behaviour during a *training event*

Hands-on Participants fully involved in working through a training *activity* themselves, rather than just being told how to do it. A key part of *participatory training*

Icebreaker An *activity* used at the start of a training event or during the day, to help participants feel more at ease with one another

In-house Training that is delivered for participants from one organization, often held in their own offices

Interactive Participants communicating with each other and taking an active part in a training *activity*

Joining instructions Details sent to participants in advance of a training event, showing timings, venue, and any preparation needed

'Known by' name The name that a participant chooses to be called by others

Learning objectives Statements that explain what a participant is expected to have learned by the end of a training session, day, or course

'Live' sessions Where separate individuals, or an identified training group, are on line at the same time with their trainer(s), and can see and hear each other

Losing face Being humiliated, embarrassed and/or less highly respected

Management committee The group responsible for running a non-profit organization. Its members are volunteers who meet regularly to take policy decisions. Also called 'council', 'executive committee', 'governing body', or 'trustees'

Mind map A visual representation of ideas, with the main topic in the centre of the page, and associated ideas and sub-ideas branching out

Name card A piece of paper/card placed on the table in front of a participant displaying their *known-by* name. Sometimes called a 'tent card'

Non-finance people Those who use financial information and systems for a part of their work

Online training Electronically providing a structured variety of materials, guidance and support to give participants the conditions in which they can learn. Sometimes called virtual training, electronic (e-)training or web-based training

Open question A question that starts with: 'what', 'why', 'when', 'how', 'where', and 'who'

Participant Someone who attends a training course. Also called a 'learner'

Participatory training Training that actively involves participants in the learning process through *hands-on* activities, discussion, and dialogue

Platform A computer based electronic communication and/or training package that can be used for one-to-one, small group training, and webinars, for example: Google Meet, Zoom, and GoToWebinar. And for longer, more formal online training courses, for example: Moodle, Teachable, Thinkific

Prop An object used as a visual aid to help make a point more memorable

Put down Embarrass or criticize someone, especially when other people are present. This could result in the person *losing face*

Road map A picture of the activities to be included in the training day or session. Usually shown at the start of the day/session and displayed throughout the training.

Saving face A way of avoiding conflict or embarrassment, and maintaining a participant's dignity and reputation, essential for many cultures. The opposite is *losing face*

Sector The part of a society or economy where an organization fits. For example, commercial (for-profit), government, and non-profit sectors

Session A section, perhaps a few hours, of a longer training event

Sticky notes A pad of small slips of coloured paper that have an adhesive strip on the back allowing them to stick to a wall or other surface

Sticky tack Soft sticky substance which, when attached to the back of paper or card, allows it to be stuck to a wall or other surface, without damage

'Talk and chalk' A training, or teaching style, where the trainer does all the talking, with little interaction from the learner. The opposite of *participatory training*

Trainer An expert on the content of the training, who will help individuals in their learning

Training event A series of *sessions* and *activities*, planned to help participants learn particular skills and/or behaviours. Also called a 'workshop' or 'course'

Welcome message A friendly and encouraging message from a trainer(s) to participants sent before in advance to tell them about the training event which they have booked

About the author

John Cammack is an adviser and consultant, trainer, coach, and writer in the non-governmental organization (NGO) sector. He was head of international finance at Oxfam and senior lecturer in accounting and financial management at Oxford Brookes University. He now works with a range of international development and relief agencies. He has worked and conducted training events in over 60 countries in Africa, Asia, Europe, the Middle East, North America, the Pacific, and South America.

His participatory face-to-face and online training includes: training trainers, developing communication between finance and non-finance staff working internationally, building non-profit management and financial capacity, and financial management for non-specialists. His consultancy work includes: programme management reviews and capacity building for European and Southern-based organizations, working with NGOs and community-based organizations (CBOs), and advising organizations on becoming 'fit for funding'.

John writes about non-profit cross-cultural communication and financial management. He is author of *Communicating Financial Management with Non-Finance People* (Practical Action Publishing), *Building Financial Management Capacity for NGOs and Community Organizations* (Practical Action Publishing), *Basic Accounting for Community Organizations and Small Groups* (Practical Action Publishing), and *Financial Management for Development* (Intrac). He co-authored *Financial Management for Emergencies* (www.fme-online.org). John is a professionally qualified manager, accountant, and teacher. He holds an MSc in International Development Management, and an MBA.

www.johncammack.net
@JohnCammacknet

CHAPTER 1
The challenges of cross-cultural training and how to respond

This chapter shows the challenges facing both trainers and participants in cross-cultural training. This can be in their own country or in other parts of the world. It offers brief responses to these challenges, and references to relevant chapters later in the book.

Keywords: cross-cultural training, participants' challenges, learning preferences, online training, response to questions, relevance of training

More and more, we work across borders, whether international, interdisciplinary, or virtual. As a result, carrying out training often means people from distinct cultures needing to work together. This offers lots of new opportunities but also new challenges. Learners who receive training in a language which is not their first, or even second, can struggle to understand the words used, as well as the training content and its cultural context. Even when people speak the same language, these same issues can be equally present.

Whether you are a professional trainer or a subject specialist with organizational knowledge, you need to know not only how to train well, but how to do so across cultural boundaries. This book will give you the essential tools to do this.

Some of the challenges for the trainer and participant are the same in all training experiences, but when training across cultures others exist too.

Challenges for the trainer

The kind of scenario outlined in Box 1.1 is not unusual for a cross-cultural trainer, travelling to deliver face-to-face training, and it can take time to understand the accepted way of working in a new culture. We will analyse these challenges and what happens in practice. We will also identify some possible responses.

http://dx.doi.org/10.3362/9781788531085.001

> **Box 1.1** A trainer's story
>
> Imagine you have flown to a city to deliver training to a large group. A driver meets you at the airport, and takes you to your guest house. You arrive just after midnight. You know the training starts later that morning, so you need a few hours' sleep. You ask the driver to collect you so you can arrive at the training venue by 08.00 to set things up.
>
> Your alarm goes off at 06.30 (though at home it is only 02.30). You have a coffee to wake you up. Soon after you get to the venue, the participants start arriving, and you continue arranging the room while they settle down.
>
> You begin at 09.00 and move into an introductory activity, using what you have prepared. You start talking and ask a few questions, but no one answers. This continues all morning. However, in the mid-morning break they all seem friendly and talkative. You wonder why they were not like this earlier.

Physical stamina

Training can be demanding for both the trainer and the participants. It is important for the trainer to build in some rest time, especially if travelling a long distance across time-zones.

Response: Give yourself at least one extra day before you start the training. This allows time to rest and to check that all the materials and equipment you need are in place before starting the course.

Need to build trust and rapport

It is important to develop a relationship with people before they will trust you. In many cultures, a trainer is treated with respect. If you are from another country or culture, it can take longer for the participants to trust that you genuinely want to work with them and help them learn. This might especially be the case if they see you as part of an organization's management. Participants can hold many preconceptions of what this means for them: for example, 'are we being judged by this person?'

Response: In the scenario in Box 1.1, it would help to greet people as they arrive, stop what you are doing and talk with them in a friendly manner. Try to remember names and use them during the course (write them down when they tell you). In some situations, you might have had some contact with people in the group in advance. Either way, spend time building trust. This might include: asking where each person is from, their work role, and something about their lives such as what family they have. In a longer formal training, it might include finding out what the participants expect from your time together, and allowing people to think together about the course 'ground rules'. For more details on building rapport, see Chapter 4, starting on page 61.

Difficulty asking questions

People may not feel confident responding to questions in front of a big group, however easy they seem.

Response: Often asking participants to talk to each other in pairs or small groups first can be a better way of encouraging them to start speaking and to build their confidence. It is easier to contribute a response after talking with a smaller group about it. Otherwise, without this safer smaller group discussion, an individual can imagine, 'I may be wrong and will look foolish if I say what I think'. For more details on asking questions see Chapter 3, starting on page 51.

Who answers questions?

In some cultures, people may expect only senior staff to answer questions. More junior staff would defer to them, even when they know more about the topic.

Response: If this happens, try to encourage everyone to participate in sharing their thoughts and finding the answer together. If the answer is incorrect, respond with 'that was not the answer I was looking for...'. Make sure you never make participants feel bad or embarrass them for contributing. Include group work as part of the training to allow participants to talk with each other, without the senior managers. Working in a smaller group can make them more confident to provide suggestions when they return to the larger group. For more details on answering questions see Chapter 3, page 51.

Challenges for the participant

Most participants will arrive with concerns (see Box 1.2). A friendly and welcoming attitude from the trainer will reassure them. Let's look at some of the participants' challenges and how we might respond:

Different work and life experiences

Participants will often have a wide range of experience from their work roles. Others will have very little. Many have experiences from outside work which could be useful for their learning, especially if you can help them make the connection.

Response: Start with the basics of the subject, so those who know little will not feel lost, and it can also be revision for those more experienced. Try to go logically through the topic and make sure everyone receives something from their learning, providing more knowledge and skills than they had when they arrived. Use any more experienced participants to

Box 1.2 A participant's story

> One of the participants spent 14 hours travelling to the training event, and arrived during the night. He had never been on a training course before, and didn't know what to expect. He was worried that he would not know what to do, and he would look foolish in front of everyone, especially his colleague who was also there. He was also worried that his English would not be good enough to understand what was happening.
>
> On the day of the training, he went to the venue early to avoid the traffic, and arrived before any of the other participants. The trainer was already there. She seemed kind and understood his English. She spoke clearly and not too fast. What a relief! The trainer started moving the tables and chairs around, and asked him to help. She thanked him several times, not something that people usually do in his culture, but he tried not to laugh.
>
> When his colleague arrived, they came and sat next to him, and expressed concern about what they might have to do. Later, the trainer came and asked the group about their jobs. He told her what he did in their office, and she was impressed with what he was doing. She said she thought the course would be very useful for his work. Maybe the next few days would be all right after all.

help teach beginners. For more details on delivering training for a mixed group see Chapter 3.

Worries about the training

Participants arrive with a variety of fears and emotions. Some worry about being embarrassed, or laughed at, if they have to speak. Training can remind them of negative experiences at school. If the trainer is from an unknown culture, this can increase participants' anxiety.

Response: Be reassuring, and create a safe and supportive atmosphere where participants realize that you will not judge them negatively. Be positive, not critical, in your approach. Tell participants that you will always start each session with the basics and build on this using a step-by-step approach – and make sure you do. For longer training events, you might include a session on 'Hopes and concerns', so everyone has an opportunity to express how they feel about the course. For some concerns, you can explain what is involved to reassure participants that they have no need to be afraid. Details of running a 'Hopes and concerns' session are shown in Chapter 10, page 193.

Concern that their colleagues will realize they do not know something

The group can all be from the same organization but at different levels within it. Participants may not want to be seen to say anything at all, especially if their manager is sitting close by; they may only feel free to talk with those from other organizations.

Response: Be careful about asking individuals for an answer in front of the rest of the group, especially in the early stages of the training. As the training develops, you should get to know the dynamics of the group, how confident each of them feels, and to identify the right time to challenge each participant. Small group work helps most participants to realize that they are not the only one that doesn't know the answer to a particular question.

Whether the course will be relevant

Participants can be asking themselves: will the training be 'too technical?' 'too basic?' or 'inappropriate for the work they do?' Some may have been waiting for this course eagerly and be desperate to know what you have to teach them. Others may have been forced to attend by their manager, possibly because they are not doing their job well. Some will not be enthusiastic, but are still willing to learn.

Response: Demonstrate how the course can be useful by answering the participants question 'what's in it for me?' Trainers need to challenge themselves with this question as well. If necessary, talk with the group about what they expect. As you go through the training put everything in the context of *why* each session will help each participant. If it does not help them, or at least some of them, ask yourself why you are including the topic. There may be a reason but be sure you, and they, know what it is.

Be willing to change some of the planned material to be more appropriate. Always try to ground the training in what happens in the real world so it is relevant to participants' needs, and explain how they can apply what they learn to their organization. You might also ask questions such as 'why do you want to attend this training?' or 'what in particular do you want to learn about?' perhaps sending a pre-course questionnaire. For more details on planning material see Chapter 3.

Will I be able to understand the trainer?

Participants can be concerned about their English language ability and feel that they will not understand what is said.

Response: Everyone needs time to 'tune in' to each other's accents and what can be a different way of speaking English. Depending on the group, trainers may need to speak more slowly than they would normally. Speak clearly and be careful not to use words or phrases that are only understandable in your home country. Trainers might sometimes misunderstand what is said by a participant, and need to ask others in the group to help. This is perfectly acceptable. For more details on

CHALLENGES OF CROSS-CULTURAL TRAINING

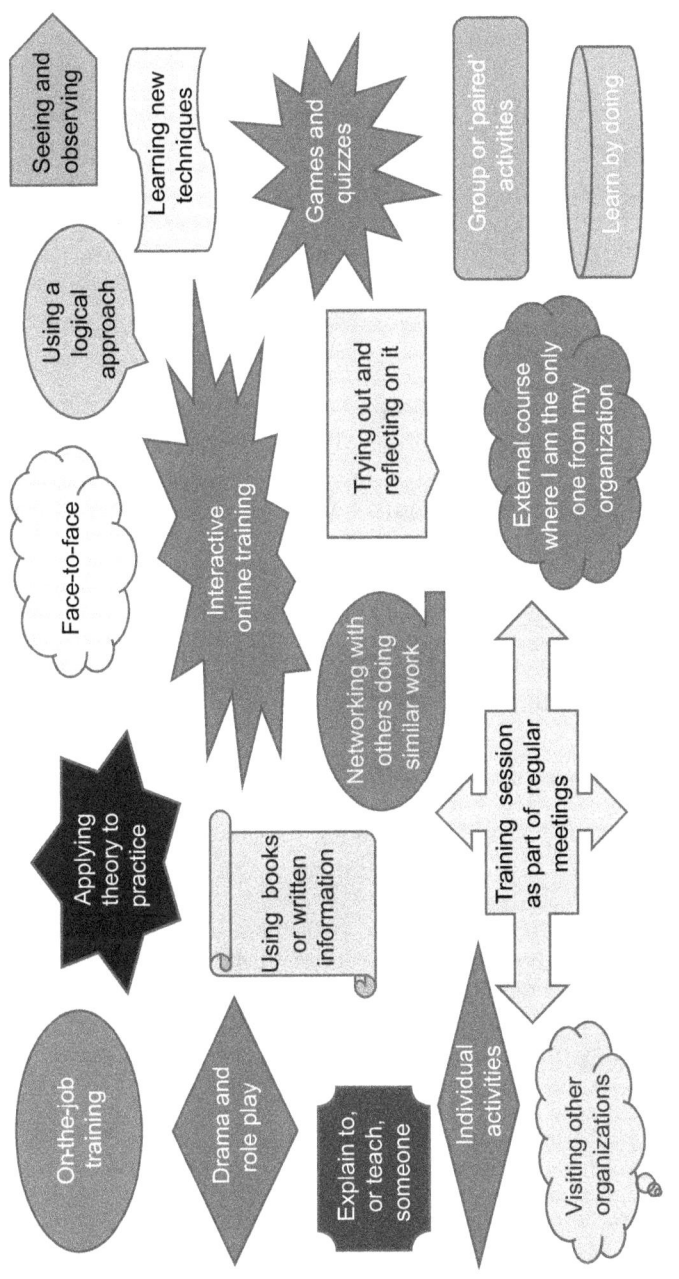

Figure 1.1 Possible responses to 'how do you prefer to learn?'

the needs of those speaking English as a second language see Chapter 3, pages 28–30.

Will the training work for me as I learn best by doing?

Everyone has a personal preference for how they learn best. If working cross-culturally, many of the participants might prefer things the training to be done in a way that they are used to. For example, in some cultures people like to see information written down and read it carefully before discussing it. Others may prefer to learn face-to-face where there is a more oral tradition.

Response: It is good to ask those involved in advance, 'How do you prefer to learn?' and list some of the choices for them to rank in order of preference. Examples of different methods of learning are shown in Figure 1.1. For more details of planning training see Chapter 3.

If you know the participants' preference, the challenge is to design the training to include these approaches. Often trainers do not know this in advance, so it is best to plan courses which include a *variety* of learning styles. Be aware of your own preferences and try not to be too biased by them.

Extra challenges with online training

When training is online, trainers and participants face many of these same challenges. These can relate to the technology, particular if the computer package, or 'platform', is new to them. Another challenge is keeping strong motivation for participants, and trainers in providing engaging materials, when they are not in the same physical space.

For more details of designing, planning and delivering, and monitoring online training, see Chapter 5.

CHAPTER 2
Understanding other cultures

This chapter looks at the cultural models of Edward T. Hall, and Fons Trompenaars and Charles Hampden-Turner. It relates these to cross-cultural training and how trainers can apply them. It ends with some useful 'dos and don'ts' when in another culture.

Keywords: high-context, low-context, professional culture, seven dimensions, saving face, cultural dos and don'ts

> Years of study have convinced me that the ultimate purpose of the study of culture is not so much the understanding of foreign culture as much as the light that study sheds on our own (Edward T. Hall).

This chapter looks at the bigger picture of culture, and offers some ways of understanding other perspectives, which differ from your own. Understanding cultural difference is essential, whether you train internationally or with colleagues from a different culture in your home office. It will look at two useful frameworks to help us understand cultural difference in a broader context and offer advice about working internationally.

It can at first seem so easy to make mistakes, but we can observe, listen, and learn. In her book *Cultural Chemistry*, Patti McCarthy (2016) uses her poem, you lost me at 'hello', to highlight a range of situations when we need to understand other cultures to make sure our communication is working and our training is effective. She is writing in a business context but it just as important in a training situation (Box 2.1).

Identifying differences in cultures

As Patti's poem shows, every culture has a different approach, and so it is always worth spending time finding out in advance. When preparing and delivering training, insights from cultural

Box 2.1 You lost me at 'hello'

> You lost me at 'hello'. From the get-go our relationship was doomed to failure, as you knew nothing about my culture, could not speak a single word of my language and were only interested in a short-term, money making exercise.
>
> You lost me because you tried to shake my hand when my religion doesn't permit me to do so. You lost me when you just took my business card and put it into your back pocket, without reading it. You lost me at our first meeting, when you proceeded to call me by my first name, as though we were old friends.
>
> You lost me when you failed to join my team at lunch, when you didn't repay the hospitality, I showed to you when you visited my country and when you opened my gift in front of other people.
>
> You lost me when you referred to my wife as the hostess and again when you sat with the soles of your feet facing me.
>
> I had such high hopes of expanding my business to another country, but you lost me by failing to understand how much these small things matter. Just because it doesn't matter to *you*, doesn't mean it doesn't matter.

Source: Extract from McCarthy, 2016

anthropology can help us to understand the background of the participants.

Avoid a 'one size fits all' approach. Instead look at the cultural context you are working in and ask colleagues from the culture(s) to give you honest feedback about what you are planning. Be prepared to adapt your approach and integrate different training styles to suit participants with different cultures from your own. Remember to respect and treat people as individuals, whatever their background.

There are two particularly well-researched groupings of cultures to think about when planning and delivering cross-cultural training. The first is 'high-context' and 'low-context' culture, and the second is the 'seven dimensions' of culture.

International cultures: 'high-context' and 'low-context'

Edward T. Hall (1989) identifies 'high-context' and 'low-context' culture to explain why people in different countries and societies communicate differently. He argues that cultures tend towards 'high-context' or 'low-context'. The main aspects of how people behave in these two contexts are shown in Table 2.1.

Table 2.1 Aspects of high- and low-context cultures

People in high-context cultures	People in low-context cultures
First establish relationships and trust, then move to the business	Start with the business and focus on the task – relationships may come later
Tend towards indirectness – people often imply and suggest things	Tend towards directness – people are explicit in what they say
Have multiple connections with others, and understand each other intuitively	Have more independence from others, with fewer shared experiences
Aim to preserve and strengthen relationships, always trying to save face	Aim to complete tasks by receiving and giving clear information
Rely more on verbal communication. Provide less written and formal information	Provide more written information and make it accessible
May say 'yes' or sometimes nothing at all, as a polite way of saying 'no'	Use 'yes' and 'no', and mean what they say
Intuitively understand without the need to use words to explain	Explain in more detail to make sure there is full understanding
Act as if there is always more time and deadlines are flexible	Act as if time is limited and deadlines are fixed

Source: Based on Cammack, 2012

A quick way to identify each culture is that:

- high-context cultures tend to 'maintain relationships at all costs';
- low-context cultures tend to 'be direct and say what they mean'.

Of course, these are broad generalizations. No one culture is all 'high' or 'low'. Certainly, people in any culture will differ from each other. A variety of experiences and cultures influences each one of us. People from a *low-context* culture might still experience a high-context culture with their families, close friends, and social groups. People from a *high-context* culture might experience a low-context culture when they are faced with public information boards, such as at an airport, instead of being able to talk with a real person. However, Hall's model helps us to understand *why* people might behave and react differently from what we expect, based on the values of their culture.

Where you fit in

Hall's ideas help us to adjust our delivery style to become more inclusive. It also helps us to prevent misunderstandings, and better interpret why a training session did not go as planned. Hall's ideas should not be seen as a shortcut to delivering effective cross-cultural training, but rather as a starting point. You need to identify which context – 'high' or 'low' – you and the participants are likely to feel closest to, and which context best describes how you and they are behaving during the training.

Many anthropologists suggest that people brought up in cultures from Africa, Eastern Europe, the Middle East, South America, South Asia, South-east Asia, Southern Europe, and the Pacific Islands, often identify as being from a high-context culture. Those from Australasia, North America and Northern Europe often identify as being from a low-context culture.

Both types of culture are equally valid. Neither one is better than the other, only different. It would also be wrong to suggest that all people from one country or culture will behave in the same way as each other. Each person is an individual with many influences. However, as the trainer, learning more about a culture is a good starting point to understand a participant's background and so improve the training's impact for them.

If you are training with participants either in or from another culture, be especially sensitive to the differences in behaviours and values that Hall's model can help explain. It is possible for all of us to be 'high' or 'low' in parts of our lives. People from different parts of the same country can show signs of either high- or low-context culture. Often people from rural areas are different to those from the cities. People belonging to certain professions too, can be seen as displaying more aspects of either high- or low-context culture, whatever their national background. Appendix 1 Self-assessment of high-context and low-context culture provides a questionnaire to offer a starting point of where you are on this cultural spectrum.

Organizational and professional cultures

Organizations have their own cultures. An international organization may reflect more strongly the culture it first started in. For example, an Indian organization that has offices throughout the world may reflect its South Asian origins, even when most of the staff are from other cultures.

Organizations may also have their own behaviours and values which employees adopt while at work. For example, an employee of a non-profit organization with a strong culture of consensus building, may practise this at work, while ignoring other people's views in their home life. Similarly, employees who work in a high-context culture may feel compelled to adopt low-context ways when working with other organizations. This 'nimble' way of moving between high- and low-context cultures is a useful skill when training and working internationally.

There can also be cultural differences between professional practices. All professions will have a mixture of approaches, but some professions can attract more low-context people, whereas others attract more high-context. Sharing the same cultural context allows shortcuts to be made when communicating technical information which may exclude others. Certainly individuals can have more similarities with someone from the same profession but from a different cultural background, than with someone from a different profession in their own country.

As an example, in the same country an accountant working with a social worker can say 'the social workers never follow the rules'. The social worker may also complain that 'I can never understand what the accountants are talking about'. The accountant comes from a low-context profession, while the social worker comes from a high-context profession. This lack of communication can damage relationships within an organization and, as a result, make it less effective.

Trainers need to learn for themselves, and train others, to communicate better between 'high-' and 'low-context' people. 'Low-context' trainers need to explain their information to a 'high-context' audience with more detail than they are used to. Equally, a 'high-context' trainer may need to be able to communicate to a 'low-context' audience more concisely and with more clarity than they are used to. This has an impact on how we design training where we often have a mixture of high- and low-context participants in the same group. Whatever the trainer's personal preference, they need to provide activities that appeal to both groups. See the 'toolkits' in Chapters 10-12.

International cultures: seven dimensions of culture

Hall's *high-context and low-context* helps us to identify the broad types of culture. A more complex picture is presented by Fons Trompenaars and Charles Hampden-Turner (2012). They provide 'seven dimensions' which help us break down aspects of particular cultures in more detail (see Figure 2.1).

We will go through each dimension to see how the different cultural approaches to life can impact on training, and how the trainer might respond to this. There are two groups in each dimension. We will look at these and what a trainer can do to respond appropriately.

1. Rules and relationships

Impact on training
- *Rules, laws, and values are more important than relationships.* The trainer explains the instructions for an activity. Participants follow these, and sometimes ask precisely what it means when you gave them a particular requirement. They may not feel comfortable working in a group with people they do not know well. They may feel less able to go into areas not in the activity.
- *Each relationship determines the rules.* Participants may decide they do not understand what you mean. They may think they do not need to follow the instructions. When they break into groups, they can be more comfortable working with each other. They might work with more initiative, but less focus on the actual activity you have given them.

What the trainer can do. Make the instructions very clear, repeat them, and check they are understood. If participants are working in a second language consider writing the instructions on a flipchart as well. Go around the groups after a few minutes

UNDERSTANDING OTHER CULTURES 15

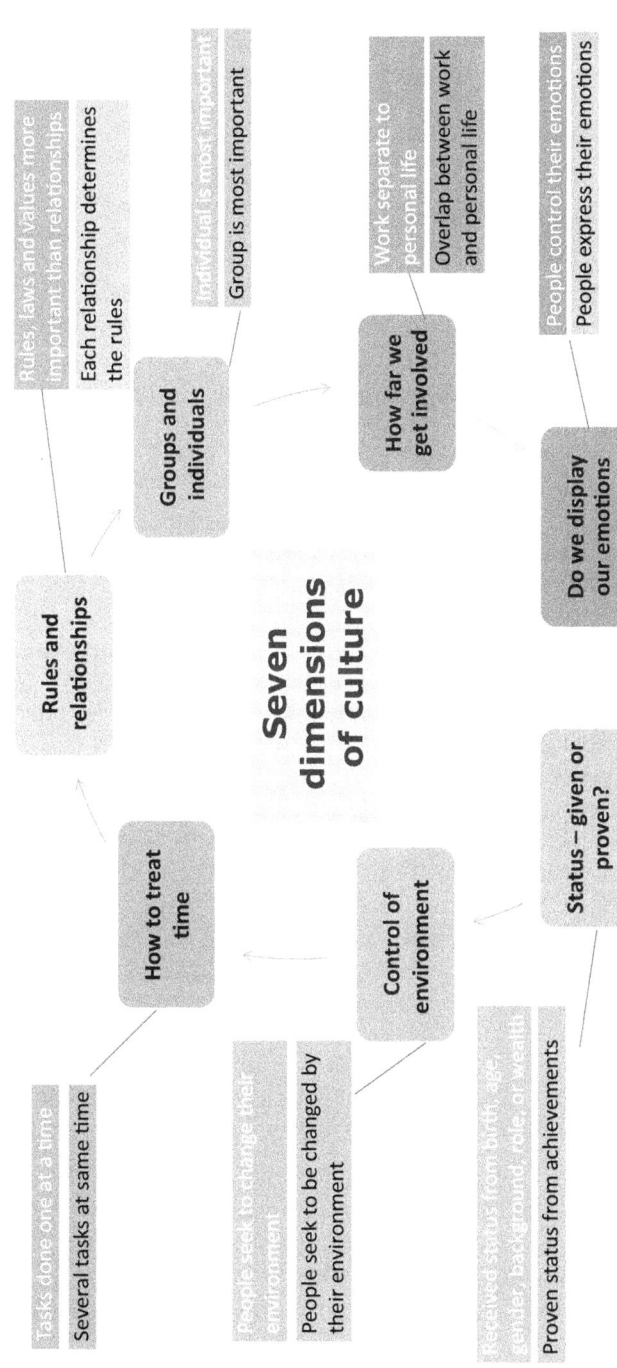

Based on: Fons Trompenaars and Charles Hampden-Turner (2012)

Figure 2.1 Seven dimensions of culture

and check that they understand what to do. Highlight any key instructions. Design training so participants do not have to follow rules, all the time. Allow some freedom and a chance to be creative, whatever the topic.

2. Groups and individuals

Impact on training
- *Individual is most important.* Participants may be happy to work within a group, but will also need opportunities to work on their own initiative.
- *Group is most important.* Cultures that are more used to working together will find group work to be quite normal. Working on their own can be more uncomfortable.

What the trainer can do. Try to achieve a balance of group and individual activities. If you need to use a lot of group work, try to mix this with activities that participants can do on their own. Participants with a strong group focus will often try to work with someone else even if you ask them to do an activity on their own. This is usually acceptable.

At the end of a group activity, ask someone to present the work of each group. Encourage everyone to present in turn, and help everyone to feel part of the group. Praise each group for all its efforts (especially when they have a strong group focus). Thank the presenters (especially when they have a strong individual focus). But if participants are highly group focused, try to avoid thanking an individual specifically, and thank the whole group instead.

3. How far we get involved

Impact on training
- *Work separate to personal life.* Participants may not want to spend all their time with each other. They will need a break from the training.
- *Overlap between work and personal life.* Participants will want to build good relationships and spend time with each other socially. They will be more likely to talk about the course without the trainer being present.

What the trainer can do. Where work and leisure do not usually overlap, do not expect participants at face-to-face trainings, to go to social activities in the evenings. Where the two more easily mix, the trainer will often be invited to social events, whatever their personal preference. Try to go to these if you can – it is usually a good experience – but do not worry too much, if you cannot.

4. Do we display our emotions

Impact on training
- *People control their emotions.* If participants are not comfortable displaying their emotions, they can seem not to be fully engaged with the training. Issues underlying their emotion can also go unresolved.
- *People express their emotions.* If participants' emotions are fully expressed, this can create an energy for the group. However, this can become unmanageable and cause disruption.

What the trainer can do. Build trust with the group throughout the course, so you have a starting point for whatever happens. With groups that display less emotion, it's important to recognize that participants may well be engaged but are not showing this on the surface. The trainer may need to provide more energy to help keep the course moving. Be careful that your own body language does not express any negative emotions. Find ways to talk with participants about any issues that may be causing problems.

If someone becomes distressed, it is wise to give all the participants a 15 minute break, so you have time to address the problem. If you are working with another trainer, you may be able to talk with the participant(s) without disrupting the rest of the training. Prior to the training event, make sure you have a plan to manage conflict.

5. Status - given or proven?

Impact on training
- *Received status from birth, age, gender, background, role, or wealth.* Those with a higher status will usually take the lead in an organization. Others will follow and find it difficult to contradict them.

- *Proven status from achievements.* Participants earn status within a group by what they can contribute to it. Everyone has an equal opportunity to show what they can give, and this is not dependent on seniority.

What the trainer can do. With a group where a few have *received status*, the trainer must respect those in authority and be careful not to embarrass them, or anyone else, publicly. The trainer should show respect by using titles if they have them. With a group of people who have *proven status*, such titles are not needed but try to recognize and value what everyone contributes.

6. Control of environment

Impact on training
- *People seek to change their environment.* The 'change' participants want to control their environment to achieve their goals. They will be happy to learn new skills to do this.
- *People seek to be changed by their environment.* The 'changed by' participants are more likely to want to adapt to their environment. They will want to collaborate with others before accepting new ways to do things in their organization.

What the trainer can do. Before suggesting changes within an organization, be aware of how participants might approach change. Make sure there is agreement from different people in an organization first, before assuming people will implement the necessary change. Allow time for them to consult more widely. Try to avoid expecting changes to be implemented as soon as you have explained it. If possible, consider having the training in two separate parts with a few days, or longer, in the middle to give time to consult. Reassure participants and try to boost their confidence.

7. How to treat time

Impact on training
- *Tasks done one at a time.* Participants are more likely to complete the task promptly and be ready for the next one. They can become impatient if other participants have not finished or the session runs for longer than expected.

- *Several tasks at the same time.* Participants are more likely to break up the different aspects of the task, and not worry if the session goes on longer than expected as a result.

What the trainer can do. Make your instructions clear and state how long is allowed for each task. Prepare additional tasks that you can ask a group to complete, if they finish before the others. If there are several parts to an activity, be flexible about how participants can complete it. Participants not arriving on time can be an issue for trainers, so remind all in the group of the importance of arriving on time. See Chapter 9, starting on page 167, *What if a participant arrives after the session has started?*

Saving face

We have looked at the two frameworks for understanding culture from Hall and from Trompenaars and Hampden-Turner. These help us to learn about culture, and can sometimes explain why our training did not go according to plan. Another important issue to be stressed in cross-cultural relationships when training is described as 'saving face'.

The overriding aim in many cultures is to avoid damaging anyone's self-image and reputation. Saving face, as this is called, is important everywhere, and especially in high-context cultures. People from some cultures even avoid attending training events for fear of losing face. This can be especially the case for an organization's senior staff, who may feel because of their seniority, they *should* know the content of the course already, even though they do not.

Beware of this issue in training events, where a trainer and participants have lots of opportunity to lose face. Be careful not to allow a situation to develop where participants are embarrassed, lose their temper, or criticize themselves, if they make a mistake.

In training events, if someone has made a mistake in what they say, help them to back down graciously. It is especially important when giving feedback on a training activity. Allowing people to save face is good practice everywhere. Participants attending a training course can feel vulnerable, especially if they are asked to participate more than they are used to. This is not a time to take advantage, or to 'put down'. Avoid disagreement and criticism, and always leave the other person a way out. Never 'push people into a corner' from which they cannot escape with dignity. Real examples of cross-cultural training situations are shown in Chapter 7.

Dos and don'ts in other cultures

If you work with people from other cultures consider the lists below. Not everything on the 'do not' list applies to every culture. However, it is best to always try to avoid them, especially if you work with lots of people from different cultures. Do not be hard on yourself if you make a mistake. Just use it as an opportunity to learn for next time. People are often more generous to their trainers than we are to ourselves. They can often be heard to say 'they are not from around here', which excuses any mistakes we might make.

Do

- be organized and be prepared;
- be courteous and polite;
- treat everyone with respect;
- show interest in other people's background;
- say positive things about the culture you are in;
- share interesting things about your own culture;
- laugh at yourself – but be careful not to put yourself down too much, as people may believe it;
- listen actively – be empathetic to the other person accepting that their world view may differ from yours;
- ask people to repeat 'what you have understood from what I have said';
- smile – this can get you out of many difficult situations;
- remember to always save face and make sure others do as well;
- be quick to say sorry;
- keep practising and learn from your mistakes.

Don't

- criticize the country you are in (or indeed any other) – even when those who live there criticize it;
- give the impression that your own culture is in any way superior to the one you are in;

- pass judgement on other people – difference does not make someone better or worse;
- become angry, which can result in a serious loss of face for you;
- be defensive – instead accept what is said and think/talk about it;
- give too much or too little eye contact – follow the lead of those you are with;
- make gestures that may mean something different to people from other cultures – it is safer not to make gestures at all;
- point – especially with your fingers, thumb, feet, or toes;
- put your feet on a table or desk;
- show the bottoms of your shoes to others;
- put your hands in your pockets;
- put your hands on your hips – it can be seen as being aggressive or impatient;
- wink – it sometimes has sexual connotations;
- cross your fingers – it can refer to a woman's genitals;
- use the 'okay' gesture, used widely in the United States, as it can be perceived as offensive in some cultures;
- give the thumbs up sign – it means different things in different cultures;
- touch a person's head – in Buddhism and Hinduism it is where the soul is – apologize if you need to reach for something near someone's head;
- whistle;
- place, or step on, books or papers on the floor – information is sometimes considered sacred;
- throw things, especially food or anything else that might be considered sacred;
- swear;
- use the name of God or a deity, or any other revered figures, in a casual or trivial way;
- use sarcasm.

More thoughts about culture

It is important to improve our cultural self-awareness, especially before meeting someone from a new culture. Try, for example, to read books, newspapers, articles, and blogs, and listen to podcasts and music from and about that culture. Talk with someone who was either brought up in that culture or knows it well. Other fun ways of learning are by going to an appropriate restaurant and watching films. Learning about a culture in advance means it is easier to understand what is happening and adapt more quickly. Always try to be open to learning about other cultures and keep reflecting on what has happened.

Sometimes training or working cross-culturally can be challenging. However, there are many benefits. For example, seeing our own culture more clearly, finding new ways of making decisions and solving problems, and understanding issues we face from different perspectives. Try to find the similarities, both professional and personal, between your own and the other person's culture. This can build a trainer's cultural awareness, and widen their perspectives, so they can deliver more effective training in future.

Do not feel you have to be perfect before you travel, have virtual contact, or facilitate a training event. If you did, no one would ever go anywhere or do anything. As long as you stay open to other people, keep practising your skills, and learn as you go, you do not need to worry even when you make mistakes. Try to become more self-aware and sensitive to other people whatever their background. Slow down, keep reflecting on your cross-cultural experiences, and look out for other people's verbal and non-verbal signals. Primarily, remember to treat each person as unique. When you meet someone, rather than thinking that this is a person from India, think 'this is Sahana', or 'this is Simon' rather than a person from the United States.

Come back to this chapter, especially when you find things are not going as well as you expect. Different cultural ways of looking at things can often explain the reason why.

CHAPTER 3

Making your training work

This chapter considers the training process in a cross-cultural context – 1) before starting, 2) designing and preparing content, 3) delivery, and 4) evaluating. It explains why using participatory methods can make training more effective.

Keywords: participatory training, training using English, learning objectives, giving instructions, presenting cross-culturally, answering questions

> *I hear and I forget, I see and I remember, I do and I understand (Chinese proverb).*

Trainers must always aim for a high standard, but this is especially important when working cross-culturally. If you are working with participants who do not speak English as their first language, and who are learning in an unfamiliar way or setting, your methodology becomes even more important. This chapter goes through the basics of training and highlights particular issues which can occur when working cross-culturally.

Training or facilitation?

Once an organization identifies a learning need, and decides that they want someone to help, they need to think about whether it really requires *training* or *facilitation*.

Training is about *developing the skills of individuals*, and facilitation is about *thinking through processes in organizations*. Both are needed at different times. It is worth exploring which of these options is most appropriate. Box 3.1 gives a definition of each.

This book is primarily about training. However, as a *trainer* issues can arise, especially if participants are from a single organization, which require you to become a *facilitator* and

http://dx.doi.org/10.3362/9781788531085.003

> **Box 3.1** What is the difference between a trainer and facilitator?
>
> **Trainer:** An expert on the content of the training, who will help individuals in their *learning*. This will usually involve *skills building* in order to improve the individual's performance. The trainer will plan the content and deliver it to make sure that *learning objectives* are achieved.
>
> **Facilitator:** Someone who works with a group to *think through* issues usually leading to *outcomes*. This may involve helping a group to learn or reach decisions, by allowing discussion, listening, questioning, and building consensus. The facilitator will usually be independent and should always be non-judgemental.

help think through a particular process. Ideally the person training can move easily between one role and the other.

Participatory training style

Participatory training involves participants in the learning process through activities, discussion, and dialogue. It is the opposite of a lecture, although the trainer will still need to have short inputs, for example by giving presentations. It is learning by doing, rather than just by listening. As the proverb says: '*I do and I understand*'. Participatory training is an important way of making cross-cultural learning accessible, and helping learners achieve the training's stated learning objectives.

The objectives usually involve participants gaining new skills, and being able to perform tasks accurately. However well the trainer talks about a topic, it will not prove that the participant is competent to perform the task. Providing 'hands-on' experience in a training event allows the person to practise, then to carry out the task in a safe environment, and receive feedback from other participants and the trainer.

Participatory methods are especially important for cross-cultural training. Listening to just words in another language is not an easy way of learning. Learning by 'doing' will often mean that the learning is better understood and is a more enjoyable experience. This approach will also make it easier to know whether an objective has been achieved, because the trainer can measure what has been learned, when seeing someone doing it.

This training style can be a new approach in many cultures where participants are used to the expert teacher just talking, rather than having much interaction with their students. If this is a different style, participants may need to be encouraged to join in. Tell them that they can ask any questions – however simple they can seem – at any time, or with you during the breaks. It is important for the trainer to treat each person with respect and value their contribution, even when it is wrong and needs gentle correction.

To achieve this kind of training means looking at all the content and asking yourself how it can be more participatory. Box 3.2 gives an example.

Box 3.2 Example of a participatory approach to training

Reviewing a topic in a non-participatory way
At the end of a few sessions about strategic planning, the trainers review what has been learned, by talking about the key points. This might not be easy for people who are not so confident in English.

A more participatory way
Give each participant small cards or 'sticky notes', ideally in lots of different colours, and a large marker pen. Ask participants to write the ideas for 'good practice for strategic planning' on the cards. The rule is to write *only one point on each card*. Each participant should end up with lots of cards. When most people have finished writing, ask each participant to place their cards on a wall or board. Then ask everyone to gather round to see what others have said. Ask two or three of the participants to put all the same or similar ideas together; ask others to help by identifying similar ones. Say that all these ideas are important, but ask 'if you were to choose just one item to introduce or prioritize in your workplace, which one would it be?' Give participants a short time to decide, and then ask each person in turn to say which one they have chosen and why.

Why is it better?
The participatory approach consolidates the learning and requires each person to engage with the review, and decide what they take back to their workplace. This increases the participants' confidence to think and commit themselves in advance to what they will change when they return.

Pretty et al. (1995) suggest some questions for trainers to think about in planning their participatory training sessions:

- How do you draw out and build upon the existing knowledge and experience of the participants?

- How long do you plan to speak before breaking up for small groups and brainstorming sessions, or for an energizer?
- Have you prepared any handouts ahead of time?
- What are the five key lessons you want participants to remember from your session?
- Have you planned the use of activities in place of someone speaking?
- Have you thought about sequencing of different training methods on one topic so they can build on each other?
- Have you decided which sections can be dropped from the planned schedule if an activity takes longer than planned?
- Have you decided how many and what size groups of participants will be needed for each activity?
- Have you decided how small groups will be formed for each activity?
- Have you allowed sufficient time in the programme for feedback?

More ideas about making online training and learning more participatory are shown in Chapter 5, starting on page 80. The remainder of the chapter is divided into four parts:

– Before the training starts
– Designing and preparing the content
– Delivering the training
– Monitoring, evaluation, and learning after the training

We will consider each one in turn.

Before the training starts

If the training is cross-cultural, the trainer is sometimes based in a different physical place to the participants. A training needs analysis (TNA) is therefore important, and it is sometimes carried out by someone other than the trainer, often a manager.

Training needs analysis (TNA)

TNA makes sure that the training targets the right material for the right people, at the right time, to achieve the required learning objectives. If the training is with one organization, someone in it needs to be sure that the training objectives are in line with its overall strategic plan. TNA identifies the gap between what an individual can do at the moment and what they need to do to perform at the expected level. A useful question to ask is, 'what do you want to be able to do differently at the end of the training?'

The training needs are often identified by a manager. This could be by observing someone in their team who is not doing their job to the required standard, or through the process of an annual staff review. The manager might then suggest appropriate training. TNA helps managers identify where these gaps are, so they can help the participants develop the skills they need to do their job. This can result in the individual feeling valued and at best increasing staff morale.

Sometimes the trainer will be asked to be involved in the TNA. Whichever way the information is gathered, it will help the trainer plan appropriate content.

Techniques for identifying what participants need can include:

- observing what happens at their workplace;
- talking with people about their expectations and challenges; and
- asking people to complete a questionnaire.

It is important to recognize that training is not always the answer. There can be organizational issues or personnel problems that need to be addressed in other ways: for example, by allocating more resources, improving managerial support support, clarifying the roles in the organization, or using the existing skills of individuals better. Sometimes the trainer has little say, other than being able to feed back to the organization what it might need to do, for example, to strengthen its systems.

Even if training will be helpful, decide what type is the most appropriate. For example, it could be on-the-job training, shadowing an experienced colleague, or self-learning using books, case studies, or online information. You could also use mentoring, coaching, an external course, or a training event held internally.

Participants' diversity

In the design of a training event, make sure that it is advertised as being open to all who would benefit from the course. This means making sure the practical arrangements and the content are accessible for a diverse range of people. This diversity includes: abilities, caste or class, culture, education, experience, faith, gender, learning styles, and sexuality. This needs to be balanced, depending on the topic, with making sure those who attend the training will benefit from it.

Make sure that the practical arrangements are in place for all participants, including access, before the training starts. Work with local contacts to make the arrangements and find out in advance who will be attending and any special needs they may have. For example, a participant may have limited sight. After talking with them, it might be helpful to prepare and give them handouts in a larger font. Try to prepare any particular documents beforehand, and consider whether it would be helpful for them to receive these in advance.

Ask participants in advance to bring along their organization's own examples of documents that relate to the content, and then use these whenever you can during the sessions. If it is not possible, look at the documents with each participant in one of the breaks and give them some feedback. This is not only important for diverse groups and in cross-cultural situations, but it always helps participants to feel it is their training event.

Training using English for second-language participants

If most participants' spoken English is at a medium to high standard. Make sure you know if everyone's English is at a similar level before the training begins, and if necessary, decide whether you need a translator. Even if participants have a high standard of English, it can become harder for them to concentrate later in the day when they are tired. Try to have more interactive material at that time. Be careful not to use slang, idioms, or metaphors, and keep asking questions to make sure the participants understand what you are saying.

If most participants' spoken English is at a poor standard. If the course has to be in English arrange for a translator, or preferably more than one, to be present throughout. Whichever standard the majority of the group are at, it is possible that one or two participants might struggle to understand. It is worth considering whether it would be useful to have a translator for them, or whether another more confident participant can act as translator when needed. Sometimes a 'co-trainer' who speaks the participants' language can be useful to explain more technical ideas.

Translation of the training for all participants may lengthen the delivery time by as much as half. Sometimes it is possible to have simultaneous translation with headphones, taking much less time, which can work well. Translators need to be of a high standard, and ideally have some knowledge of the subject area. In all cases, it is worth letting a translator see any written materials you will use at least a few days before the training starts. If only certain participants need translation, and headphones are not used, it is helpful to place those participants and the translator at the other side of the room from the presenter to avoid the other sounds disturbing either of them.

Sometimes all participants speak the same language. Sometimes a variety of languages are spoken. The following points will help you to communicate well in writing or verbally whatever the training situation:

- Keep your speaking clear and simple using plain English. Use whole sentences, while keeping them as short as possible.
- Avoid long, complicated instructions (see Box 3.5, page 43).
- Repeat key information in a number of different ways. Speak just slightly slower than in ordinary conversation.
- Show facial expressions and body language that support what you are saying. Use visual clues if you can.
- Avoid using phrases or references from your own culture when the meaning is not clear. An example is 'to dip one's toe into the water' meaning approach something cautiously.
- Be careful with words that have different meanings in different part of the world. Summer and winter, for example, depend on which hemisphere you are in.
- Try to avoid jargon words, unless there is a common understanding with these particular participants. Always

explain the meaning of any technical terms, whatever the English-language ability of the group. People often struggle with these terms, in a second language, even if they are well qualified in the topic.
- Provide written materials, ideally in a booklet, in plain English to back up the training. A glossary will also be helpful. Participants will often study this booklet in the evening, and it is useful to fill in gaps that people could not understand in a particular session. They will often then ask the trainer questions about the topic the following day.
- Write key words and ideas on a large sheet of paper. Display this throughout the training. Be willing to go over the material again, and include regular reviews of what has been covered. Find fun ways for learners to remember what they have learned.
- Try to present things visually, rather than always using words. Write down instructions as well as speaking them. Written words are easier to understand in a second language. Use images to explain and support some of the key ideas.
- Allow plenty of time for the participants to work together in small groups. If everyone speaks the same first language in the group, it will be easier for them and allow them to concentrate more on course content. It also helps involve those who are less confident.

Expectations in advance

Before the training event, and ideally before you start to plan the course in detail, find out what is expected from the training. After initial discussions with the organizer of the training, and seeing the TNA, you may want to show each of the different areas you intend to cover. Ask the organizer to rank these in terms of their importance to them. You might also list learning styles (see Chapter 1) and ask participants to rank these, giving a one for their most preferred topic/style, two for the second and so on.

Writing learning objectives

Using all the advance feedback from the organizer and the participants, and your own experience, you can put together learning objectives and a day-to-day programme that is likely to target their training needs. You can consult with the local organizer of the training, or perhaps a manager, to check whether this covers the right topics. Sometimes people 'don't know what they don't know' so the trainer then has to take responsibility for this.

Learning objectives are sentences that describe each of the learning topics. They focus on what the learner will be able to *do* rather than what they will *know* or *understand*, by the end of the training. These need to tie in with any TNA, and often can be seen as filling the 'gaps' between how participants currently do things, and how they should be done after the training has taken place. The following two examples from a training of trainers course show how learning objectives are usually written:

By the end of this training, the learner should be able to:

- write clear learning objectives and training plans to achieve desired competency;
- plan and deliver a participatory training session confidently.

Objectives are written using 'active' verbs – for example write, compare, prepare – at the start of each objective. Words such as 'know', 'understand', 'appreciate', or 'realize' should be avoided as they are difficult to observe or to measure. A key question is whether we can measure that the learner has achieved a particular objective. This is made easier when an active verb is used in the objective. In the objectives shown above, you could ask to see someone's written objectives and training plans; and observe them delivering the training. Having written an objective, it makes it easier for the trainer to plan and deliver material that will help learners achieve it. Also, importantly, the training participants will know what is aimed for, and later the trainer can ask them whether it has been achieved.

A good way of testing the effectiveness of your learning objectives is to see if they are 'SMART'. This stands for:

Specific. Does it precisely describe the learning objective?
Measurable. Can you say 'yes' or 'no' to whether someone has achieved it?
Attainable. Is it possible to achieve the objective in the time available, even though it may stretch the participant?

Relevant. Is the objective relevant to the overall topic of the training and for those attending?
Time-bound. What is the time limit to achieve the objective?

Using these criteria, we can look at the two learning objectives shown above to see how SMART they are:

- Write clear learning objectives and training plans to achieve desired competency.
  Is this SMART? Yes, because it is:
  Specific. It says to 'write clear learning objectives and training plans'.
  Measurable. It is possible to see these documents, and judge whether they are clear.
  Attainable. It could be completed during the course.
  Relevant. Trainers need to write these.
  Time-bound. To be completed 'by the end of the training'.
- Plan and deliver a participatory training session confidently.
  Is this SMART? Yes, because it is:
  Specific. 'Plan and deliver' says what is required.
  Measurable. It is possible to judge how confidently it is prepared and delivered.
  Attainable. The should make this possible.
  Relevant. It is a key requirement of a training of trainers course.
  Time-bound. 'By the end of the training'.

If you are inviting external people to a training event, these learning objectives, together with a list of the topics to be covered, show potential participants what they will be able to do by the end of the course. This approach makes it more likely that the people who will benefit most, will be the ones who attend. For a list of action verbs to use when writing learning objectives see the Appendix, Table A.2. Also, see the References and resources section at the end of this book for links to information about learning objectives.

Welcome message

Participants can be anxious about what will be involved in a training course. Along with sending them the joining instructions and any pre-course materials, try to reassure them that the course content, style, and structure will not be threatening. The 'welcome message' is a way of doing this. It also makes it easier when participants arrive at the start, as they already know something about how the training will proceed and already have a connection with the trainer. Add details of anything you want the participants to bring along with them, such as documents from their own organization.

If the training is for participants who speak English as a second language, you may want to show you are aware of this (and possibly translate the welcome message into their language). You could also let them know whether there will be a translator available or, if not, explain the situation by saying 'I realize that some of the participants speak English as a second language, so I will make sure throughout that everyone is following the course material'. An example of a welcome message for a one-day course is shown in Box 3.3.

Box 3.3 Example of a 'welcome message' for participants

Fundraising for Beginners

I am very much looking forward to welcoming you to our course *Fundraising for Beginners*. I thought you may like to see the outline programme for the day:

Welcome and introduction
'Whistle-stop' tour of fundraising
Creating a proposal and budget to tell a story
Effective ways of presenting what your organization does
Avoiding what can go wrong
Learning log and feedback

The course is introductory and will start with the basics. Don't worry if you feel you don't have any experience of fundraising – you won't be asked to do anything that you don't feel comfortable with.

The style will be participatory with a balance of short inputs, discussion, group work, games, and individual activities. There'll be lots of opportunities to ask questions.

As preparation, if you have a chance, take a look at a fundraising proposal you have access to, possibly from your own organization. If possible, bring a copy of it with you. If you have a calculator, bring that. Otherwise just bring yourself.

Let me know if there is anything you are worried about. I am looking forward to meeting and working with you.

(Your name), Trainer

Importance of structure

A clear course structure will help participants to see what they are working towards. Provide participants with a written agenda for the whole training event that shows what it will include, session by session. Try to send it in advance with the joining instructions and the welcome message. This is especially helpful for those whose first language is not English. Do not change the structure unless absolutely necessary, but if you do, let the participants know.

Prepare in advance and let your host know what you need

Training can be sitting with one other person informally, or it could be a formal training event. In either case, and certainly if a trainer is in one part of the world while the learners are in another, the trainer must let the local contact know, in advance, what they will need. The format in Box 3.4 gives a concise way of saying this and to make sure nothing is forgotten. This example has been completed for a two-day strategic planning training event.

Training supplies

Generally, you can expect your local contact or host organization to provide a flip chart stand with enough paper and marker pens, and a projector and screen. Sometimes there will be a laptop, too. If you want to show an online audio or video clip make sure you have a good internet connection or, if possible, download the clips in advance. If you want to show a DVD make sure the equipment will play the version you have. It is always wise to check exactly what facilities and equipment will be available in advance. Take smaller things with you. For example, marker pens in a range of colours, coloured card, sticky notes, sticky tape, and sticky tack. Your host might not have them or run out before the training event ends, and you may not be near anywhere that sells them or the quality is not always good. A helpful rule is to make sure you have all the essential supplies you might need for the training, or at the very least for the first day of the training event.

Box 3.4 Example of a training requirements format

Training course: Strategic planning. Dates: 2–3 December	
Layout and equipment:	
Room layout:	In groups of four gathered around tables and facing the front
Equipment:	Flip chart – stand and three paper pads (if possible two stands)
	Laptop
	Projector and screen
	4 packs of sticky notes, if possible, in different colours
	Sticky tack, sticky tape, stapler and hole punch. Note pad and pen for each participant
	Marker pens (one for each participant and set for the trainer, cards (five for each participant)
Special access needs:	None for the trainer
Dietary requirements:	Vegetarian

Copying instructions:
- All documents will be printed on A4 paper, in black and white, and double-sided, unless stated otherwise.
- Documents of multiple pages will be stapled unless stated otherwise.
- PowerPoint presentations will be printed as '6 slides per page' unless stated otherwise.

Documents for copying

Document title	Instructions for copying	Quantities
Agenda for the training	Double sided	1 per person
Handbook for the course	Print as a booklet stapled down left side	1 per person
PowerPoint copies	Single sheet – four slides only	1 per person
Top tips in strategy	Double sided – two pages	1 per person
Case study 1	Double sided and stapled together – four pages	1 per person
Case study 2	Single sheet	1 per person
Evaluation sheet	Single sheet	1 per person
	Please include a copy of each document for the trainer	
	Original documents have been sent in a separate email	

Participants' packs [in the order needed/filed]

Document Title	Instructions	Quantities
Agenda for the training	Include at top of the pack	1 per person
Handbook for the course	Second in the pack	1 per person
PowerPoint copies	Third in the pack	1 per person
Evaluation sheet	Fourth in the pack	1 per person
	All other documents will be handed out during the training	

Equipment required by trainer

Item	Instructions	Quantities
Remote control	For projector	1

DVDs

Document title	Instructions
'Being strategic for beginners'	Required in the morning of second day. Please check if the video equipment will play a DVD from Kenya.

Source: Based on an original document prepared by Bond UK, used with permission.

Designing and preparing the content

Designing and planning each session

After you have gathered the training needs, and you have written down the learning objectives, identify the time and other resources you will have. Find out about the participants – their genders, culture, backgrounds, current roles, physical abilities, preferred ways of learning, and their level of English. Work out the number of sessions available and which topic to focus on in each session. You will need to structure the sessions to make sure each one builds on what has come before.

Once you have the main topic for a session, the next step is to design the content of it in detail. A process that will help with this is called 'mind-mapping'.

Mind-mapping is a tool that helps generate ideas and organize training. It involves laying out all the key ideas visually and making logical connections between them. Having thought through the sequence of a session, it will make it easier for both you and the participants to follow step-by-step what you are doing and why. When you have a clear idea of how everything in a topic connects, you will be in a stronger position to explain these connections to participants, especially those from other cultures. Figure 3.1 summarizes how to mind-map.

Make all the sessions as participatory as you can. Plan to talk for no more than about 10 minutes at a time. Even then involve the group, for example by asking questions, and provide activities for the group that will help them to learn. Allow plenty of time to create new materials, case studies, and background information to fit the specific training needs.

Required: a sheet of paper and some different coloured pens
1. Write the main topic in the centre of the paper.
2. Add the component parts of the central topic around it on the page – represent possible training content using images, words, and symbols.
3. Add further sub-sections of these key parts.
4. Use lines to show a connection between ideas – thick ones from the main idea and thinner ones as the ideas expand outwards.

Remember:
- Put key words in CAPITALS.
- Include linked words in lower case.
- Use colours to help group ideas together.
- Leave lots of space so you can add more later.
- Do not think too much, just let the ideas flow from your brain.

Figure 3.1 Example of mind-mapping a training session

Before you send anything off for photocopying, ask someone to read it through and give you feedback.

Logical order

When you have created the material, make sure it is arranged so that each session builds on what has come before. This will make it easier for participants to learn.

Timing

The design of the sessions needs to make the most of the time you have. Recognize that you will not be able to include everything. Remember to prioritize the material. Make sure you include extra time for breaks, talkative participants, and questions and answers. Also, take into consideration that if working with people who are less confident with English, the sessions may take longer than you expect, and even more so if you use a translator.

Think about the best time of day to present each session. Although you want the material to follow on logically from the previous session, certain times of day can work better. Participants concentrate best later in the morning, so present your most complex material then. Make sure the sessions in the early afternoon are interactive as participants often become sleepy, especially after a cooked lunch. Towards the end of the day when the group will be tired, the trainer could present more entertaining material with lots of fun and energy. If you have had a session that the participants might find challenging, try to follow it with a lighter session with some material that they will find more straightforward. For example, after a technical session when participants perhaps feel 'I'll never understand this', move on to something that they can do easily to reassure them. Sometimes, presenting a short video clip is a good way of helping to switch the mood and can be more relaxing for the trainer as well.

Preparing your presentations

Even in the most participatory of training events, it will be necessary for the facilitator to present information to a group.

It may be about a new topic, an explanation of a technique to develop skills, or trying to change behaviour in a work situation. In preparation for a presentation, you should:

1. Decide on the objective, if not already written in your learning objectives.
2. Assess what the group already knows about the topic – or if in doubt, ask them.
3. Gather together all the necessary documents and information.
4. Recognize the amount of time available.
5. Prioritize what you include. Use the 'must know', 'should know', or 'could know' technique. Concentrate on the 'must know'. It is usually better to cover a limited amount of material fully, rather than try to include everything, but more briefly (see Figure 3.2).
6. Identify your key message.
7. Structure your presentation logically, making it easier to follow.

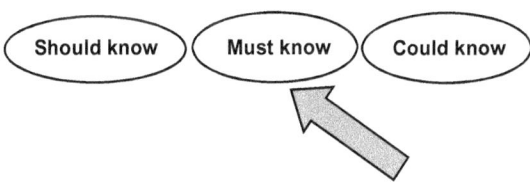

Figure 3.2 How to prioritize training content

Training plans

In addition to the agenda, prepare a more detailed training plan for each day with a summary of what you will cover. It keeps all the information about objectives, timing, materials needed, and methodology on one sheet for yourself and any other trainers to refer to. An example of a training plan is shown in Table 3.1.

'Hands-on' learning

Participants need to have materials to work through during the training activities. You could provide them, but it is even

Table 3.1 Example of a training plan

Training of trainers – plan for day 1 morning

Overall course aim: to build participants' confidence in using participatory training skills.

Session 1 - Key learning objective:
At the end of the sessions, participants should be able to:
- commit themselves to the expectations and rules of the training;
- recognize the challenges in training and learning and identify how to respond to them.

Topic	Content/key points	Methodology	Materials	Timing
1. Introduction to the course	Welcome and introductions	Welcome	–	5 minutes
		Introductions activity	Flipchart	30 minutes
		Identify expectations in small groups, then bring together on flip chart and discuss	Flipchart	20 minutes
2. 'Ground rules' of the course	Basic details • reassure participants about methodology	Talk by trainer and questions and answer sheet	Programme for training	10 minutes
	Ground rules of the course • make sure rules are 'owned' by the group	Write ideas on sticky notes, working in pairs, then fours to identify rules agreed by the whole group. Participants put sticky notes on flip chart and discuss	Handbook Sticky notes.	25 minutes
	Home groups	Form home groups and short discussion	Paper/pens	15 minutes

(continues)

Topic	Content/key points	Methodology	Materials	Timing
3. Challenges of training adults	Identify challenges and ways of responding • bring out particular challenges	Each group draws the challenges as a picture Each group thinks of ways of responding Share with larger group and discussion	Paper/pens Handbook	25 minutes
	How to deal with 'sabotage' in courses • recognizing the techniques for dealing with saboteurs	'Saboteur' game and discussion	Chairs Session handout	20 minutes
Morning break				*20 minutes*
4. Responses to challenges of training	Motivation for and benefits of learning • reasons for people attending and ways group dynamics can shape course	Group activity and feedback on flip chart	Sticky notes	45 minutes
	Quotation game • reviewing wisdom about training • importance of participation	Each participant identifies wisdom from motivational quotes in training displayed around the room. Each participant chooses their favourite and says why they like it	Handbook Posters showing quotations	20 minutes

better if they can bring real examples from their organizations and receive your feedback. If it's a fundraising course, have them write an actual proposal they could use. For financial training, ask them to interpret a real budget report. A recruitment workshop could use real application forms (with all personal data blanked out) and let individuals conduct mock interviews. If this is not possible, write a case study and allow groups to come up with a list of what they would do in a real situation. For numerical activities, give participants a copy of the solution. This will aid their learning.

Planning activities

Use case studies and examples that reflect the diversity of the group. Avoid stereotypes of people. For example, make sure that any roles included in case studies have a mixture of male and female names, and names that represent a mix of cultures. References to place names should be familiar to participants and drawn from their country and cultures. Ideally, ask someone from the participants' cultures to read the materials before they are copied and give you feedback. If cutting and pasting from an existing document, make sure you have updated all the names before copying.

Good preparation

Everything needs to be ready in advance, at least the day before the training event starts. Take a back-up version of all your materials. Occasionally materials you send by email are lost, or are not presented quite how you wanted. For example, a copy of the solution may be printed on the back of the activity, or one important item may not have been copied at all. If you have your own back-up version to copy from it's much easier to produce more when you arrive. There may be an office nearby, with copying facilities, but not always.

Delivering the training

All the time you spend designing and preparing is for the purpose of delivering the training. In most cultures, there is a lot of goodwill towards the trainer, and participants want you to succeed. However, there are a number of cross-cultural issues to be aware of, particularly in how you present yourself so that participants can understand you. This section explores some of these issues and suggests how to make your communication as effective as possible.

It is important when working cross-culturally for participants to understand clearly what you want them to do. This applies to all parts of your delivery. Participants can easily misunderstand if they are listening in a second language, and when the instructions are about complex issues and tasks. Box 3.5 gives some guidance.

Box 3.5 Giving instructions when working across cultures

- Tell the participants what you are going to do.
- Display brief instructions visually and, if possible, in the training materials as well.
- When giving instructions verbally, say them several times in different ways. Then ask 'is there anything more you need to know about the task before we begin?'
- Ask if one of the participants could summarize what you have to do, to check their understanding. Gently correct any misunderstanding.
- After a few minutes of work, check briefly with each group to see if they need any more information about what they should be doing.
- When starting off an activity with many possible answers, offer a first idea to clarify what you are looking for. For example, if asking small groups to produce a list of good practice for managing a project, you could suggest 'to have regular monitoring' as the first item.
- If it is a written or numerical activity, the framework of the solution might be written down for them to complete and, if possible, one part already completed.
- Ask 'open' questions that start with 'what', 'why', 'when', 'how', 'where', and 'who'. Avoid 'closed' questions that only require 'yes' and 'no' responses.
- Tell participants how long they have for an activity, and what reporting back they need to prepare (if any) and then add 'all right, let's start'.

Arrival activity

After participants are welcomed to a training event it is good to have something for them to do as everyone gathers and before you start formally. Possible options include having quotations about the topics of the training placed on the walls around the room, asking participants to choose their favourite. They could reveal their choice when they introduce themselves to the group later. Another idea would be to have a flip chart with space for participants to write a number. For example, the number of days they have been with the organization (for induction training) or the number of years they have been involved in fundraising (for more experienced staff attending training about a particular topic).

Starting a training event

How you open the course will depend on which culture the participants are from. In some cultures, the opening of a training course can be a formal event (and sometimes the closing too). Important guests are invited and speeches are made. This can sometimes take several hours. Afterwards, it is useful to have a break so the guests can be thanked properly, before the training begins. Ask your local contact if there is anything planned for the opening and adjust your timing accordingly.

However, when the event starts, you may like to have a list of what you want to say with you. This helps you not to miss anything out, and may give you more confidence to start things off well. Make sure you turn off any distractions, such as projectors, before you begin to speak. Usually pressing the letter 'B' on the keyboard will turn off the image, and then pressing any key will turn it back on. This will mean that the participants' attention is on you, making it easier to create a connection with the audience.

Practical information

After the welcome for participants, there is often practical information to share. For example, the start and finish times, what happens if there is a fire, and where the toilets are. You could display some points participants need to know on a poster or flip chart page. An example of this is shown in Figure 3.3.

You could also write 'welcome' in their first language or languages on this poster, if this is not English. As people arrive, you could then check with them that you have written it correctly. Another alternative would be to find a poster or a projected image with 'welcome' in many languages.

MAKING YOUR TRAINING WORK 45

Figure 3.3 Example of a welcome poster

Try to keep this practical information brief, rather than just going through a mass of information, which can lose participants' engagement before the training actually starts. One participatory way would be to give participants the information written down and ask people to sing the words shown to an internationally well-known tune, such as 'Happy birthday to you', or a song of the group's choosing. You could divide into several groups and ask each group to sing a verse each. It's great fun and something they are likely to remember!

Expectations

You may have received information from the participants about what they would like to cover in the training. This is useful, but can be incomplete and not everyone may have contributed. It is worth spending some time at the start of the training to ask participants for their expectations and put them together in a flip chart list to display throughout. Try to adapt the training to include these expectations of what they will learn, if you can. Be clear and manage them so you do not promise what is not possible. If an expectation is outside the scope of the training tell the participants. Let them know where they might go to find more, following on from the training. Refer back to the list of expectations towards the end of the training and make sure everything has been met, or if not, agree what to do about it. See Chapter 10 for *introductory activities* which can be used at the start of a training event.

Hopes and concerns

As discussed in Chapter 1, participants will arrive at the training event with both hopes and concerns about what the training will be like. For everyone to make full use of the training, it can be helpful to address these on the first morning. Ask participants to think about how they would like the training to be, and what they are worried about. See Chapter 10, page 193 for an introductory activity about 'Hopes and concerns'.

Structure of the day and a 'road map'

A visual 'road map' lays out the structure of the day's activities in detail on a large sheet of paper (see Figure 3.4). Show that day's road map to the group at the start of each day, and refer to it at the beginning of each session. It helps to put the day in context. Display it prominently for each day of the training.

Delivering your presentations

Start with the basics, even if this is brief, and then progress to more advanced material. Many groups will include some who know a lot and some less.

Try to use points that build on each other and provide evidence for what you are saying. Having identified the key points for your presentation, think if it is possible to use some participatory approaches, even if it is just by asking the group questions. You will generally need an introduction, main body, and conclusion even for a short presentation. When you have this structure, you need to make them what John Collins (1998) calls 'an exciting start, a logical middle and a memorable end'. The start is very important as it has to grab and hold people's attention. The ending of any session can be what participants will remember most clearly, so make sure it

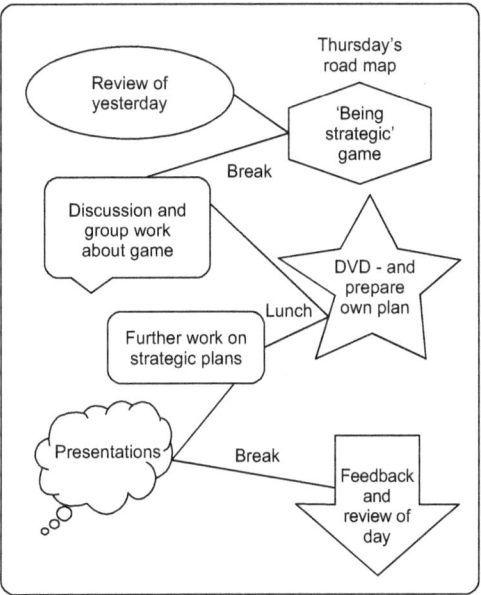

Figure 3.4 Example of a 'road map'

contains your key messages. Rehearse and memorize as much as you can, but especially the beginning and ending.

As you are speaking, verbally 'signpost' when one section ends and the next begins. For example, say 'we have so far looked at why we need a strategy, let's now move on to what needs to be in the strategy'. Showing the individual sections visually also helps participants to follow more easily.

Try not to fill every second of your presentation with sound. Do not be afraid to be silent. Feel free to consult your notes if you need to. It is more than all right to say something such as 'let me just check that I have covered everything you need to know'. Then pause while you do, and say 'yes that's about it' or 'oh yes, there's just one more important point I want to tell you about'. Silence can also be a sign that you are comfortable with the group (especially in parts of Africa), or that you are showing them respect (especially in parts of Asia).

Be aware of *how* you speak and how it sounds to others. If you are unsure, ask a friend to listen to you and give you some feedback. Make sure you articulate well, with each word clearly spoken in full. Try to vary the pace at which you talk, and the pitch, tone, and volume of your voice. Express the enthusiasm you have for the subject through the sound of your voice.

Make presentations that engage all your audience's senses: sight, smell, sound, taste, and touch. Use interesting images, appropriate clips from YouTube, and stories with clear but captivating words as you speak. Find relevant objects as examples to pass around for the participants to hold. Sight especially is the strongest sense to help people remember what you are communicating.

You might also like to film some of your presentations and then watch them back. This is the quickest way to see your strengths and weaknesses as a trainer, and how to improve. Box 3.6 gives a summary of dos and don'ts when presenting.

Using visual aids

Think carefully about handouts and visual aids in advance, and whether you need them. If you do use them, consider whether anything needs to be translated. Participants' learning can be dramatically increased by seeing words in their own language. However, translation means you will probably need to have both English and another language on the page or slide, which will take up more space. Pictures, photos, and diagrams can often be more effective than words. Try to find appropriate images, so you can use fewer words. You can also use film clips from online sites to add variety.

If you are projecting images:

- create a landscape format, which is easier to read;
- use a minimum 20-point font size;
- include different colours and shapes to highlight particular words – see an example on page 7, figure 1.1;
- use colours and text which contrast well with the background colour;
- cut out as many words as you can.

When presenting with a projected image:

- look at the participants, not at the screen;
- make sure everyone can see the screen and do not block anyone's view;

Box 3.6 Dos and don'ts of presenting

Do
- prepare your presentation thoroughly;
- make sure all the content is suitable for a cross-cultural audience;
- tell stories to keep the participants' attention, to connect with them, and to stir their imaginations;
- share your passion and be enthusiastic about your topic – have fun while keeping your credibility;
- start with the 'big picture' of the topic and why it is important, before going into the detail;
- include a clear memorable beginning and end for each block of information;
- repeat your key messages several times and keep them simple;
- give clear 'signposts' of where you are, have been, and are going;
- pause slightly, before saying any unusual words, names, or technical terms – and show these visually as well;
- prioritize the key points – concentrate on the 'must know';
- use participatory techniques as much as possible;
- ask the participants questions, and answer their questions;
- use visual aids – pictures, quotations, props – to reinforce your message;
- vary your pitch, pace, tone, and volume to hold participants' attention;
- speak clearly in plain English and in complete sentences as much as you can;
- smile and make appropriate eye contact and so relate to everyone in the group;
- move your position in the room – move nearer to an individual if you want to create a closer relationship, or further back to give a sense of authority within the group;
- keep observing how the group is reacting to you – especially their body language – and change your approach if necessary, perhaps by getting them to discuss a topic in pairs or small groups;
- look confident and relaxed – even if you do not feel it;
- give out a clear, attractive handout to back up what you are saying.

Don't
- include everything you know about the topic – three main points is enough;
- go over the time allowed;
- shout;
- be afraid of silence;
- use 'non-words' in the presentation such as: 'um', 'er', 'like', 'I mean', 'you know';
- speak too fast, or too slow;
- use jargon without explaining it, or abbreviations – instead say the words in full;
- read from a projected slide – keep content of all slides to a minimum;
- stand in front of visual images;
- have any physical barriers between you and the group, such as a laptop or lectern;
- use gestures unless you are sure they do not mean something else to the participants.

- turn off the screen when it is not in use – press the 'B' key on the keyboard;
- decide in advance what you will do if the power goes off in the middle of the presentation.

Projected images should be used to illustrate what you are saying. The focus should be on *you* and what you are saying. If you have a flip chart available, writing up key words and technical terms can be very effective.

Use other visual aids as well, sometimes called 'props'. These are objects that reinforce what you are saying, and they can also be fun. You can also display posters and written flip charts. People will often look at these throughout the training and it will help to reinforce the learning.

Handouts

Give participants concise, clearly written handouts. They can then use them to refresh what they have learned in the future. If possible, present them in one 'handbook' for the whole training (except the solutions to activities). If you give the handbook out at the start of the training, it will help participants with English as a second language, to follow more easily. If you have case studies, activities, and numerical questions, you can give the solutions as separate handouts, after the activity.

- *Design.* Present the handbook in colour with plenty of white space around the text. Use diagrams, bulleted lists, and pictures to illustrate and make the content more attractive. Design the handbook logically, in line with the content of the training. Make sure the heading, sub-heading, and fonts are consistent throughout.
- *Ease of use, especially for English second language speakers.* Write the handbook in plain English and in a lively style, with a glossary to explain any technical terms. Include activities with the written instructions. This will make it much easier to read.
- *Content.* Provide references to books or articles for following up the topics and an up-to-date list of useful websites. If possible, find resources from the countries where the participants

live and show how to obtain published materials there, for example the contact details of publishers' agents. Remember to show the source of any part of the materials which are not your own so participants can follow up on these ideas too.

Inclusiveness

When speaking at a training event, use local examples that reflect the experience of the participants. Always use inclusive language and avoid stereotypes and prejudiced statements. Discourage and stop participants using any language which is racist, sexist, or homophobic. If there are particular issues about inclusiveness which arise in the course, you may need to return to the ground rules put together at the beginning of the training. See Chapter 4, page 65.

Questions and answers

Questions from the trainer are a vital part of the learning process. They help participants to think, challenge their assumptions, and boost their awareness. It is best to use open questions, starting with 'what' and 'why', 'when' and 'how', 'where' and 'who' rather than closed questions that need a 'yes' or 'no' answer. Such questions have the potential for participants to explore issues, challenge their assumptions, and change their current ways of thinking, rather than simply responding without thinking about the 'right' answer.

In some cultures, for example in Asia, the answer to a closed question will always be 'yes', or sometimes nothing at all. For example, if you ask 'do you understand this?' it can be considered rude to say 'no', as it implies you have not done a good job at explaining. Try making it an open question asking them *'how* would you summarize what we have just learned?' Or ask someone to to 'teach' you what they have just learned.

Regularly invite questions from the group and listen carefully, not only to the spoken question, but also what lies behind it. As a trainer, you can help the group to arrive at answers to their own questions, by asking 'what do you think the answer could be?' or 'can anyone else help to answer this question?' This increases the participants' confidence and helps them to take more responsibility for their own learning. It can also inform your own answer. If you consider that the group are reluctant to ask questions individually, ask them to take a minute or two to think up a question in pairs. This then gives the questioner more confidence.

In many cultures, the trainer is assumed to know all the answers. Of course, this is impossible, but this assumption can reduce the questioner's ability to think for themselves. It can imply that they will always need an expert. The trainer can not always know the answer. In *some* cultures, the trainer would be seen negatively if they do not answer. In *other* cultures, it would seem foolish, and possibly dangerous, if they gave an incorrect answer to avoid 'losing face'.

As a compromise, respond by saying 'that's a helpful question, but I want to check to make sure I'm absolutely right before I give you an answer. I'll come back to you later'. Then make sure you do! One technique to help with this is to put a sheet of paper on the wall with a title 'parking space'. Explain in the introduction to the training that 'this is a place to write (park) questions or topics to come back to later'. This can include topics which the group can follow up for themselves, especially during 'in-house' courses. Any other questions are there as a reminder to the trainer and participants that they need answering.

In all cultures, allow participants to avoid losing face, however silly their question is. This may not only embarrass the participant but, in the eyes of the group, it could diminish respect for a trainer who has allowed this to happen.

Boxes 3.7 and 3.8 summarize what to do and what not to do when asking and answering questions.

There are more ideas about design and delivery of training, working with groups, and asking and answering questions in Chapter 9, 'Training cross-culturally: frequently asked questions'.

A good ending

A good ending to a training event is just as important as a good beginning. Make sure the 'ending time' celebrates what has been learned, but also the shared experience. This is especially important in cultures that prioritize the group over the individual. Stay with the participants until they have all departed – it is good way of answering any final questions and possibly talking about future training options for them. Try to avoid taking down posters or clearing things up until everyone has left. Ideas for course endings are shown in Chapter 12, 'Concluding activities'.

Box 3.7 Dos and don'ts when *asking* questions

Do
- Use open-ended questions, starting with 'who' and 'what', 'when' and 'where', and 'how' and 'why'.
- Pause after you have asked the question, to wait for the answer.
- Pause and be prepared for silence when asking questions – wait about 10 seconds, look around the group and then check again, saying 'any ideas?'
- Listen carefully to each response and its meaning.
- If there is confusion about the question you have asked, say 'tell me what you think I am asking?' and then clarify.
- Write the question on the flip chart if it will make it easier to understand.
- Ask a basic question to the group to increase its confidence, before asking a specific question that builds on that knowledge.

Don't
- Use closed questions which need a 'yes' or 'no' answer very often. Participants will often say yes automatically. It is not a good way of checking understanding.
- Imply the expected response in the question you ask.
- Ask two questions in one – for example 'how would you explain and summarize for us?' Ask two separate questions.
- Ask multiple questions at once – such as 'what do you know about the best way to fundraise? Who are the major funders? and 'How do you tell them your strengths?' Instead ask each question separately.
- Ask questions with a negative in them – for example 'why don't you think this is a good example?' instead say 'why do you think this is a good example?'
- Use jargon that some participants may not understand.
- Use vague or imprecise words in your question – 'substantial', 'everyone', 'things'.
- Use slang words (for example instead of 'dodgy' use a more widely understood word such as 'unreliable').
- Use acronyms (for example instead of 'UNHCR' say 'United Nations High Commissioner for Refugees').
- Use idioms (for example instead of 'cut corners' say 'to save money').

Box 3.8 Dos and don'ts when *answering* questions

Do
- Make it clear early in the session when you will answer participants' questions – either as you go along, or at the end of the session or both.
- Be as prepared as you can for expected questions.
- Listen carefully, and do not interrupt the question.
- Repeat the question for the rest of the group, if they may not be able to hear.
- Paraphrase the question if it is not concise or clear, and check with the questioner that the meaning is still correct. For example, 'am I right in thinking you are asking…?'
- If the question is unfocused, ask the questioner to clarify what the question is.
- Check body language as a clue to someone wanting to ask a question, and then ask gently 'did you want to ask something?'
- Thank participants when they ask questions.
- Pause before responding to a question, both to allow you to think and to put emphasis on your answer.
- Look at the issue from a different perspective, if participants are finding it difficult.
- Be concise in your answer and try to refer back to your presentation.
- Ask the group if they have experiences relevant to the question.
- Check that the question has been answered satisfactorily.
- Make eye contact with the whole group, not just the questioner, when answering.
- Answer all questions, even if briefly, rather than saying 'we will cover this later'. If appropriate after the answer then say 'we will look at this in more detail later today'.
- Answer someone who makes a comment rather than asking a question by just acknowledging it – for example 'that's a good point, thank you'.

Don't
- Let anyone lose face, including yourself.
- Give long answers – if needed, say 'we can talk some more about this during the break'.
- Use jargon that some may not understand.
- Be patronizing to the questioner, using words such as 'obviously', 'you should', 'you must' – it may discourage others from asking questions.

Monitoring, evaluation, and learning after the training

Monitoring during the training

Do not leave gathering participants' feedback until the end of a formal training event. If you do, it will too late to respond to any concerns. Instead, ask for feedback as you go through the training. For a one-day training, do this at the end of the morning. For longer training events, at the end of each day. Be sensitive to any suggestions, and if possible, adapt the rest of the training. Possible ways of gathering feedback are:

1. Ask 'how is it going?'
   - *The pace.* What does it feel like? (is it too fast? too slow? about right?)
   - *The content.* How are you finding it? (is it too simple? too advanced?)
   - *The English.* How well can you understand me/us? (speaking too fast? too slow? how clear is it?)
   - *Other issues.* Is there anything else the group want to feed back?
2. Ask for comments on a flip chart. Prepare a flip chart with two headings: *'I like...'* and *'Could be improved...'*. Put numbers 1, 2, 3 below each column heading. Ask the group to work together and write up three points for each. Leave the room while they do this. After they have finished, come back to formally finish the session. When they have left, use the lists to see if you need to adapt anything. If there is a major concern, discuss it with the group at the start of the next session.

   A similar approach is to give each participant some sticky notes. Ask everyone to write one *'I like...'* and one *'Could be improved...'* and place them on the top or bottom half of the flip chart.
3. Have a sheet with three *'smiley' faces* on it. One happy, one neutral, and one sad. Ask people to place a tick against the one that represents how they are feeling about the training. This is a quick way of knowing how well your material is being received.

4. For training events of several days, make use of the *expectations* completed and written up on the first day (see page 45–46). Draw participants' attention to what they said, and ask which ones have already been met – put a tick by these. Then consider what is still to be done, and how it could be fitted in to the time left. Prioritize if you

need to. You can ask if there is anything else that the group wish to add to the previous expectations.
5. At the start of a longer course, divide participants into groups, one for each training day. Each day ask one of these groups to *gather feedback* from all the participants, and then sit with you for 10 minutes or so at the end of the training. They then present their comments so you hear directly how they feel the training is going, and discuss any changes needed. You also have an opportunity to raise anything.

Evaluation

At the end of the training, participants are often expected to complete an 'evaluation form'. This gives feedback about the training. Some of these questions require participants to tick a box, perhaps on a scale of 1 to 10, 1 being very poor and 10 excellent. Other questions should give an opportunity for a written response. This can be helpful for trainers to develop their approaches and materials.

The evaluation form is often required by the organization offering the training, and sometimes by its donors too, if the training is externally funded. Individual trainers are often not involved in the design of these forms. However, if you are designing your own form, you could ask questions such as:

- How well did the training meet your expectations?
- How well were the learning objectives fulfilled? (specifying the main ones).
- How relevant was the training for your work?
- What sessions were the most valuable?
- What sessions were the least valuable and how could they be improved?
- What was the most important thing you learned?
- How will you put the learning into practice?
- How will you pass on what you have learned to others?
- How effective was the trainer in helping you to learn?
- How well did the training methods used suit your preferred learning style?
- How would you rate the administration of the training?
- How would you rate the training overall?

Extra questions to add when training across language and cultural boundaries might be:

- How easy was it for you to understand the trainer's English?
- How well did the trainer understand your culture?
- What would have made the training more appropriate for someone from your culture?

When you read these evaluation comments at the end of a training event, there are likely to be negative as well as positive ones. You might like to go through them with a colleague to find a more detached perspective on what they are saying. Alternatively leave it a day or two, until you are more emotionally separated from the training and have a better perspective yourself. Give yourself time to reflect and be willing to adjust your training, if needed.

Often especially with participants whose first language is not English, a written feedback form is more straightforward. However, there are alternative ways to obtain feedback, such as:

1. Simply ask towards the end of the course 'would anyone like to say how they have found the training?'
2. Use *storytelling* as a way of letting participants and the trainer review, and express, how the experience of the training was for them, in a fun and safe way (see Chapter 4, page 66).
3. Ask participants a month or two after the training, what impact it has had on their behaviour and work. One key question to ask is 'what difference has the training made to your work?' It gives you a chance to look again at the learning objectives and see if they feel they have really been achieved. This takes more effort, but provides a fuller picture. It is ideally carried out face-to-face, but if not, by telephone or online. Asking by email or social media can also be useful.
4. A number of free and commercially available apps will allow participants to complete an evaluation using their cell/mobile phone or other device. This will sometimes process the results as well and save training administrators a lot of time. Search for 'training poll app' to find a number of choices.

Trainers may also want to ask themselves questions after the course, to learn from the experience for their personal development. These can be questions such as:
- What went well?
- How well did I achieve the learning objectives?
- How well did I achieve the organization's aims for the training?
- What could I do better next time?
- What did I learn about cultures through delivering the training?
- How do I need to change the materials and presentations ready for next time?

Further learning after the training

Help participants to put into practice what they have learned in their place of work by:

- *Sending them additional information.* The trainer can send some useful additional materials a week or two after the event. This may include any documents that were promised at the training, together with a few other handouts that expand on the training. It also maintains an important link with the trainer for possible future training needs. If everyone agrees, it can be useful for participants to share their contact details with each other. This allows them to support each other as they put the learning into practice.
- *Having follow-up sessions.* To maximize the learning, it may be possible to arrange one or more follow-up sessions with the trainer. Depending on the content, these can be arranged some weeks or months later. Check with the organization funding the training when negotiating the event, and if this would be beneficial, see if their budget can stretch to this. Box 3.9 gives an example of how follow-up might happen.
- *Visiting participants after the training.* A training session may be followed by a visit from the trainer to each participant's organization. This could be a few weeks after the training event, to make sure each participant is happy with the new systems that have been established. It will help them consolidate and integrate the learning to their place of work.

Box 3.9 Story: training and follow-up

> The Copperbelt Health Education Project (CHEP) provides workshops for the communities it works with in basic financial skills, resource mobilization, and management of income-generating activities. The financial workshops cover topics such as completing accounting documents and cash/bank books, preparing bank reconciliations, and compiling financial reports to donors.
>
> At the end of each workshop, the participants complete an action plan of tasks to carry out when they return to their organization. During the meeting to review the action plan after the workshop, CHEP's staff check progress on agreed tasks. For example: 'Establishing an equipment register in the format taught during the training'. CHEP staff follow up this training with 'mentoring' and 'monitoring' visits to each of the participants.
>
> The *mentoring* visit usually takes place two weeks after the workshop. It aims to discover whether the training has been effective in the participant's work situation. A typical visit would check that documentation exists for every stage of ordering. The organization is helped to develop its project proposals. They are also taught how to manage small business initiatives to contribute to their sustainability.
>
> After the first mentoring visit, there are follow-up *monitoring* visits to make sure that things are running smoothly. Further visits, phone conversations, and online contact are then arranged for as long as needed afterwards.

Source: Copperbelt Health Education Project, Zambia, extract based on Cammack, 2014

This will be a more expensive option, but can improve the quality of their work significantly. A trainer could then act as a mentor for a fixed period, even if undertaking this at a distance. If this is not possible, an email or phone call after the training 'just to see how you are getting on' can also be useful.

- *Create a social media group where participants can share how they implement the course learning.* You might want to create a social media group before the course begins, and use it to distribute joining instructions, as well as information during the course. After the course, participants can use it to share how they feel about implementing the materials, what their colleagues' response was, and how it has all worked out. This can capture some of the spirit of the course, and maintain the group support that you established in it. You can ask participants to record a short video on their thoughts about the course which with their permission, can be used in marketing of future training.

- *Reporting back on the learning from a training event.* All training should be used as an opportunity to pass on the learning to others who were not able to participate. Encourage them to report back to their own team or organization when they return. Not only is it helpful to their team, but it reinforces the learning for the individuals. They can do this with a written or verbal report about the training. If possible, learning materials can be copied and shared (if copyright rules allow or permission is sought). To encourage this practice, it is good for trainers to include the question 'how will you pass on what you have learned to others?' on the training evaluation form.

Additional aspects of these topics when training online, are shown in Chapter 5.

More thoughts on training

If you have planned and delivered training before, much of this chapter will be familiar. If not, a lot of this will be new to you. You are invited to use as many of the ideas as you can. However, if you are learning how to train as well as learning to train cross-culturally do not be critical of yourself. Instead, celebrate what goes well and learn from what does not. If you can, ask a trusted colleague with more training experience to give you some honest feedback. Above all, enjoy the experience of being a trainer.

CHAPTER 4
Practical techniques for training cross-culturally

This chapter provides practical techniques for cross-cultural training. It offers suggestions for the trainer, including how to build rapport with participants, remember names, and set ground rules.

Keywords: building rapport, remembering names, ground rules, drama in training, storytelling, keeping time

> *Teaching is only demonstrating that it is possible; learning is making it possible for yourself (Paulo Coelho).*

In Chapter 3, we considered the stages of developing and delivering the process and content of training. The aim of this chapter is to offer practical techniques for training cross-culturally. Many of the approaches are good practice in all training, but become increasingly important when working across cultures.

There are three sections: *welcoming*, *content*, and *practical arrangements* (see Figure 4.1). Some of the suggestions can be adapted for other work situations, and in your private life.

Welcoming: helping participants feel comfortable
Building rapport

Building rapport starts when you welcome participants to the training event. It is an essential foundation for making cross-cultural learning effective and enjoyable. Make sure that all the practical arrangements are in place early enough so you are free when they arrive. Be open and friendly, and help them to feel relaxed. If possible, find out how to do this in a culturally appropriate way by talking with a local contact or

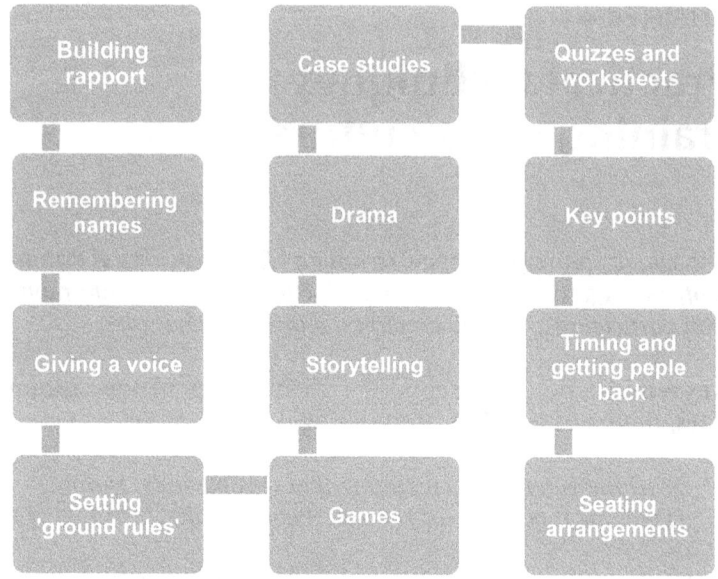

Figure 4.1 Welcome, content, and practical approaches

reading about the culture. Some examples are given in each of the country profiles in Chapter 7 starting on page 103.

Be attentive to what participants say as they introduce themselves at the beginning of the first session. As you introduce yourself, establish your own credibility, and the reason that you are well-placed to facilitate the training, without sounding superior. Make some eye contact; however, be aware of what is the normal level of eye contact in the culture(s) you are in. This might be more or less than you are used to.

As the course progresses continue building rapport by:

- using your body language to show that you are relaxed and open, for example by not crossing arms or legs;
- 'mirroring' the body language of the other person subtly, and trying to use some of the same words that they use;
- making sure no one is left on their own during group activities or energizers, and be ready to step in as their partner, if needed;

- helping a participant to catch up if they miss part of a session;
- using participants' names when you talk with them;
- acknowledging everyone's input – refer back to a participant's contribution in an earlier session to show that they have been heard and valued;
- making sure the timing of breaks and endings of sessions are respected, to help the participants trust the trainer and keep the rapport going;
- showing participants that you are interested in how they will use the learning to benefit their organizations and the people they are serving;
- always 'saving face' – yours and theirs.

Remembering names

If you are working with a group that is new to you, try to remember people's names. If you are in a familiar culture this can be relatively easy. In an unfamiliar culture, you may not have heard the names used before and you might find them difficult to remember and pronounce. Matching these names to the right person can be challenging but is important to try. The following steps can be useful:

- Ask the person organizing the training to send you names in advance and, if possible, photographs of the participants. Not everyone may be happy for you to have their photograph, so do not leave these visible in the training room.
- Familiarize yourself with the names, and with the pronunciation, before the training starts.
- When you greet each participant personally, ask them what they would like to be known by and its pronunciation. Write the name down.
- If you are unsure of your pronunciation, you can ask 'am I saying your name correctly?' This gives the participant the chance to correct you. If you forget, you can ask again.
- When the first session starts, ask people to say their name to everyone in the group and to write what they like to be called – their 'known by name' – on a folded piece of card which they then place in front of them.

- At some point early on in the training, sketch a plan, for yourself, to show where each participant sits. You might like to add a code to remember a feature about the person. For example, make up a code for something distinctive – for example G for glasses, T for tall, C for curly hair, and so on.
- Ask participants to stay in their original seats, apart from working in groups, until you are more familiar with their names.
- Use participants' names every so often throughout the training to help you remember them and to build rapport.
- An advantage of online training is that some platforms have the participants name on screen to help us remember. Make sure though that is really is their name, rather than the name of the person who owns the devise they are using.

Giving a voice

In most groups, there will be participants who are confident talking in front of others and those who say little. When training in another culture, it can be difficult to know what is happening within the group. For example, if the training is with people from the same organization, you may assume that the most senior person present will speak on behalf of everyone.

The trainer's job is to create a safe space for all. Sometimes, this may mean, during one of the breaks, sensitively asking the most talkative participants to allow others a chance to contribute. Make sure the more talkative or dominant participants are not always in the same groups. You may sometimes want to put them in a group by themselves.

At other times, you can ask a less talkative person a question, especially if you know they have valuable experience to share. Invite participants to contribute rather than demanding an answer, to lower the risk of their losing face. Prompt these participants if they are unsure how to respond. Use lots of paired and group work where individuals can, more confidently, express their views to a smaller audience first. Encourage different participants to present a group's findings each time, but do recognize this might be difficult for some, so be careful not to put too much pressure on anyone.

Content

Setting ground rules

Having everyone agree the ground rules for a training event is a good way of making sure there are shared expectations of behaviour between participants and trainers. They should be completed towards the beginning of the training and need to answer the question 'how do we want to work together?' Ask participants for ideas and discuss them as a group. Issues raised are likely to be about being on time for all sessions, turning all mobile/cell phones off, maintaining confidentiality of anything discussed during the training, and being open to all suggestions and new ideas.

If the training takes a day or less, it can be a fairly minimal. For training events lasting several days, it is worth spending time for participants to agree their own ground rules. Break the participants into groups of three or four, and ask them to make a list. Their rules should aim to be clear and memorable. After this, ask each group to rank their top three items. Then go around, asking each group in turn for their number one item. When all the groups have been asked, do the same for item number two, and then number three after that. Write these up on the flip chart. Many will be the same as other groups, so include them only once, but put a tick by them each time the rule is mentioned again. The trainer can add their suggestions if something important has been missed. Display the list where everyone can see it for the rest of the training. Tell the group everyone is responsible for keeping the rules. If there is a dispute, take the discussion back to the whole group.

Games

Games are a fun way of learning. They can be used when participants are tired, or after they have struggled with challenging material. With groups who have limited English, try to have more straightforward games that do not rely too much on words, and where the instructions are brief. Try to include something in the game that has a connection to the training topic, while still being fun. Also, be aware of participants' physical abilities and cultural preferences, including gender.

Choose a game which all can join. See Chapters 10, 11 and 12 for examples of *introductory activities, energizing activities,* and *concluding activities,* respectively.

There are many published training simulations, games, and activities that can be used as part of learning, and some free ones. The *Resources section* at the end of the book includes links to printed and electronic sources. If you cannot find a suitable one, try writing your own!

Storytelling

Most cultures love to tell stories. This is a great way of building rapport, consolidating learning, and having fun. Stories can also create empathy and shock us into action. They are a good way of communicating a participant's experience and allowing them to talk about sensitive topics. Storytelling can be an effective way of working across professional and cultural divides. If telling personal stories, remind everyone that what happens in the group must remain strictly confidential. A storytelling activity is included in Chapter 12, starting on page 204.

Drama

Acting out a story can be a powerful way of communicating and bringing about behavioural change. Most cultures use drama to portray behaviour and its consequences and to help an audience to reflect on what they have seen.

The trainer could write a short dialogue, or sketch, which can be acted out. Better still, invite the participants to take part, and you could ask them to write the dialogue themselves. This might need some preparation beforehand. If so, give them some guidance and time for preparation during the training. However, not every group will be happy to act out a dialogue that has not been fully rehearsed. Be sensitive to this and be prepared to change the approach, if needed. At the end of the drama, lead a discussion drawing out the main points.

An alternative is to give participants a description of a particular situation. This could be real or imaginary, with clearly defined characters. Give each character a name, a role, and a goal for them to achieve in the situation. Participants are then invited to volunteer to take on those roles. They then improvise a scene between them for a given amount of time.

For example, a representative from a funder comes to visit and assess an organization. The characters in it are: the funder's representative, the organization's director, and the chair of trustees. Other members of the group act as observers and make notes – give them points to look for, such as 'what happened?', 'how did the various characters relate to each other?', 'how can we interpret their body language?', 'how did they come to a conclusion?' and 'how could it have been done in a different way?'

Lead a discussion afterwards to see what the participants felt. Start the discussion by asking those who played the characters, questions such as 'how did it feel playing that role?', 'what do you think went well?' and 'what would you do differently next time?' Then ask the observers for their comments. At the end, the trainer should help those involved to come out of character. When ready, they go back to being an ordinary member of the group.

Sometimes participants feel comfortable acting out the situation in small groups of three or four. This is less threatening and there may be some useful insights from the different approaches within each small group. These insights can be drawn out in the discussion.

With dramatic activities, be careful not to use the words 'role play'. Many people freeze when they hear those words, and will not then be happy to participate. Instead, describe it by saying something like: 'I want us to try acting out a situation'. Encourage participants to have a go but do not force anyone. Use drama only when you have built good relationships and enough trust within a group, so not on the first day. If possible, you could ask a local contact how appropriate they think using drama would be.

Case studies

A case study presents a real or imagined challenging situation. Participants read, analyse, and come up with solutions for it, usually in small groups. A case study helps to translate new ideas and skills into the participants' experience, using real examples. To make sure this happens, the case needs to be something that all participants can relate to. Include names and places appropriate for the country and region you are in. Make sure the description is brief, clearly written, and in plain language. At the end of the case study description, add concise questions that you want the group to discuss. When introducing it, state how much time is available and how participants will report back.

Quizzes and worksheets

Written quizzes and activities are often easier for those with English as a second language, as they can see the questions. You can use a formatted worksheet that is partially completed to give a structure. If you use multiple-choice questions, participants may find this easier.

Key points

Ask yourself what messages you want the group to remember. Repeat important points in a number of different ways, and then summarize them at the end of a session, and the course. People will often remember these points if everything else is forgotten. Make the key points stand out in the way you present them. For example, you may want to explain the most important thing for a manager to do when change is happening. You could stand on a chair and say 'communicate, communicate, communicate, communicate, communicate'. This visual picture will be memorable in a way that words alone will not. Chose your 'chair' equivalent, and make your message impossible to forget.

Practical arrangements

Timing and getting people back

Try using fun ways to make sure participants come back after a break on time. For example, you could make a noise with a whistle, a bicycle horn, or a bell. Just before you have a break, state the time you will restart, and ask someone to be responsible for making sure participants return ready for the next session, giving them the whistle, horn, or bell. Ask a member of the group who knows the culture well to do this. If you will not disturb others in the building, you could use some music from the culture(s) of the group to say it is time to start the session. See Chapter 9, starting at 183 for more issues about timing when delivering training.

Seating arrangements

Sometimes the trainer has little choice about how the seating is arranged but, if you can, arrange the chairs in a way that will encourage a participatory approach. Try to avoid rows of chairs all facing the trainer at the front, unless this is the only way everyone can fit in the room. Ideally, everyone should be able to see each other. A circle or semi-circle of chairs can signal equality and make interaction easier. It also means the space is more flexible. However, there is no surface to work on and participants can feel intimidated. For training topics that require a lot of writing, one option is to have tables dotted around the room in a way that everyone can see each other. Alternatively, arrange the tables as three sides of a rectangle, with the trainer presenting from the fourth side.

For more practical techniques, see Chapter 9 for frequently asked questions about training cross-culturally, and the toolkits in Chapters 10–12, for introductory, energizing, and concluding activities to use in your training.

CHAPTER 5
Planning and delivering cross-cultural online training

This chapter looks at the advantages and disadvantages of planning and delivering cross-cultural training online. It shows when and how this differs from face-to-face training as well as how it can still be delivered in a participatory way. It will look at the types of online training, dealing with the technology, ways of encouraging participants' engagement, and it also includes a checklist to start your 'live' online training sessions.

Keywords: online training, e-training, types of online training, participatory cross-cultural online training, online training practicalities

> *Learning is more effective when it is an active rather than a passive process (Kurt Lewin).*

With the recent pandemic and the effects of climate change already happening, we need to look again at how necessary and possible it is for us to travel, and the effect it has on our planet. It will still be necessary to have face-to-face training inside and outside our own culture and country, but online training and learning is becoming an increasingly viable alternative. In addition to all the points in the previous chapters, focusing on what is happening from a cross-cultural perspective becomes even more important online where misunderstandings can easily occur. Online training can also be used to improve participants' learning experience by using additional features. It can be cost-effective too.

What is online training and learning?

> Online training provides a structured variety of materials, guidance, and support to give participants the conditions in which they can learn.

http://dx.doi.org/10.3362/9781788531085.005

Online training (also called virtual, web-based, electronic or e-training) is delivered using a simple online communication or a specialized training platform. The most important question to ask is whether potential participants will have access to the internet. This can be through any device, although a small screen may make it difficult to easily view complex information. In many countries, internet connection strength can vary, especially in participants' own homes. Often, however, an employer will be happy to let participants use their organization's online facilities, either in or out of working hours.

Advantages and disadvantages of online training

There are a range of advantages and disadvantages of online training. For example, courses can sometimes be more easily accessible than face-to-face training, for those for whom English is not their first language. But a high degree of motivation is required from learners, especially if they are working and studying over several weeks. The advantages and disadvantages of cross-cultural online training, compared with face-to-face learning, are summarized in Box 5.1.

Types of online training

As with face-to-face, an online course is likely to be addressing a particular organizational need, possibly following a training needs analysis (TNA). Following this you can decide what form the training should take and, if delivered online, the platform or combination of platforms that would work best. The types of online training include:

- *One-to-one training.* This might be described as training or 'a conversation', for example between an individual employee and their manager. It could be about a single issue. Ideally those involved would be able to see each other, but if necessary, it could be delivered through audio alone.
- *Seminar.* A group of people, typically with a presentation followed by questions and discussion.
- *Webinar.* Delivered as a visual presentation about a particular topic. It involves some participation.

Box 5.1 Summary of advantages and disadvantages of cross-cultural online training

Advantages
- Possible to attend training from anywhere in the world regardless of location or physical limitations
- Participants with less fluent English may find it easier to see as well as hear information
- Improves access, for example, by including transcripts and subtitles for recorded presentations
- Training materials can be translated into participants' first language(s)
- Lower cost, with no travel, accommodation or venue expenses
- Participants can usually progress at their own pace
- Easier to repeat parts that are not fully understood
- Can have easy online access to supporting materials while learning, such as a glossary
- On some platforms, everyone's name appears on screen making them easier to remember
- Some participants can be more confident when interacting with a screen rather than in an actual training room

Disadvantages
- Participants need more self-motivation to learn
- Reliant on the trainers and participants having a good internet connection
- For longer courses, participants are often juggling work and study
- Learning to use new platforms and developing appropriate materials can take a lot of the trainer's time, and so can be costly
- Difficult to make sure everyone is engaging at the same pace
- Harder for trainers to absorb the culture(s) if not there in person
- Picking up non-verbal signals is much more difficult
- Difficult to have a sensitive conversation with a participant
- Building confidence of some participants may be less possible than with face-to-face training

- *Online training course.* Specific structured training course delivered through a learning platform perhaps over 4 to 6 weeks.
- *Blended learning.* Includes a mixture of online and face-to-face training, perhaps over a longer period.

Table 5.1 on pages 75–77 summarizes the features of each of these training and learning options. The online resources, starting on page 215, contain links to websites that compare the different platforms available for training, learning, and online communication.

Online training can include a number of these methods combined. The first three of these types can be delivered as single, stand-alone training events, but can also be a way of bringing together trainers and participants as part of a longer training event. An online training course and blended learning can include, for example, weekly 'live' events as a way of connecting with each other, answering questions, supporting learners, and increasing motivation. The rest of this chapter looks at live events mostly as part of these longer training courses.

Getting the practicalities right

The technology

The initial fears that many trainers have about online training are about being responsible for the technical aspects of the platform but also the subject content and delivery. It is important to know the technology well or, if not, have someone who can help you with this. Ways to build up your confidence include: practising using the platform before the start of the training event, or signing up to another online event using the same training platform to see how it feels to be a participant.

Make sure that your connection, as well as that of any other trainers involved, is the best it can be for live training events. You may want to use an Ethernet cable to connect your PC, laptop or tablet to the router rather than Wi-Fi for a more reliable signal. If you are using the internet regularly for training, it is worth experimenting to find which part of the building has the strongest signal. If working from home, try to make sure that no one else is using the internet at the same time as you, to minimize the possibility of the system being overloaded. Games especially can reduce your connection strength. Close everything else on your device that you do not need.

Check that your device is fully charged or plugged into a mains supply, and that batteries in your remote mouse do not need replacing. Trainers and participants may be in a country with possible power cuts, so try to have a plan in case that happens. In countries with poorer internet connections, using their video link may reduce the quality of the audio and, at worst, the connection may be lost altogether. So, it is important to be flexible.

Table 5.1 Summary of online training and learning delivery options

	One-to-one training	Seminar	Webinar	Online training course	Blended learning
What it is	A 'live' structured training or coaching session, or just a 'conversation'	A 'live' session for teams or individuals to learn together about a specific topic	A 'live' structured presentation with a question and answer session	A mix of interactive materials to study and activities to perform. Ideally supported by 'live' events with a trainer(s)	A mixture of online materials, interactive activities, and 'live' events. It also includes a few face-to-face training events
Possible number of participants	One-to-one, or possibly a small group. If any more, would need to use a stronger platform	Two or more, up to the limit imposed by the platform	Five or more, up to the limit imposed by the platform	6 to 15 in one group – if less, group interaction is harder; if more, difficult to tailor the sessions to everyone's needs	6 to 15 in one group; many groups possible with the same materials
Typical timing	1 to 2 hours	1 to 2 hours	1 to 2 hours	Often a stated number of weekly hours over 4–6 weeks, but can be longer	From a few weeks to a year
Type of learning platform	Internet-based audio and/or video	Internet-based video	Platform that allows learner participation	Platform specifically for training	Platform specifically for training
Possible participation	Questions and answers, sharing screens, using 'reactions'	Shared screens, using 'reactions', can often break into groups	Shared screens, a poll of participants in answer to a question, visual 'reactions'	Lots of possibilities. Can often replicate face-to-face methodology	Lots. Benefit of knowing each participant online from face-to-face meetings

Table 5.1 (Continued)

	One-to-one training	Seminar	Webinar	Online training course	Blended learning
Trainer/ facilitator needed?	Either, or could be a manager/ staff member	Either, but needs someone to 'facilitate' the session	Either, or just a presenter with someone else to manage questions and the administration	Either, ideally someone who can do both to maximize the group potential	Trainer and facilitator, may also be a 'personal tutor'
Time needed for the trainer(s) to prepare?	Depends on the topic, typically 1 to 2 hours	Depends on the topic, typically 1 to 2 hours	Often a visual presentation takes several hours to prepare	At least as long as face-to-face training, and extra time needed to become familiar with the technical aspects	Large amount, but can be worth it if the training is delivered many times
Need for learning objectives?	Yes, if structured training	Yes, if structured training	Yes	Yes – detailed	Yes – detailed
Need for participant motivation?	Low	Medium	Medium	High	Very high
Social media support?	Not usually	Not usually	Can be added to maximize the learning	Yes, and facilities for 'forums' for participants to share ideas	Essential, 'forums' and regular contact between participants
Peer support?	If more than one learner	Sometimes	Sometimes	Yes – essential for learning	Essential and easier if participants have already met in person

Table 5.1 (Continued)

	One-to-one training	Seminar	Webinar	Online training course	Blended learning
Assessment?	Not usually	Not usually	No	Yes, as a way of giving feedback and assessing that learning objectives have been met	Yes, essential to achieve learning objectives and give regular feedback
Advantages	Low or no cost. Easy to organize. Can share the trainer's screen	Low cost, easy to organize. Some participation possible	Gives information in a structured way to a large number of people. A recording is usually available	Time consuming, but for the trainer the number of 'live' events is spread over several weeks part-time	Can provide longer and more intense learning experience
Disadvantages	Can have technical problems. Participation limited	Participation may still be limited	Cost of the platform used. It can be mostly one-way training from the presenter	Technical costs are high for platform and its development. Can be low motivation from participants	Technical costs are high for platform and its development. Extra costs for face-to-face events

Finally, review the security of the platform you are planning to use. Check the security advice of the platform provider beforehand, and consult social media for recent advice from the platform's users. If it is a live event, make sure there are no unauthorized users attending.

Your visual presence

Think about how you want to be seen on the screen. A good rule is to wear the same clothing as you would in the training room. Avoid touching your face, eating or drinking, other than a glass of water. Remember participants are sat there mostly just watching you!

When talking, try to look at the camera which will then show that you are looking at the participant. Be aware though of how much eye contact the cultures of the group are used to, which may be more or less than your own. If you are reading a script on the screen you are not looking directly at the camera, so try to remember what you are going to say, particularly the beginning and end of the session.

Think about the background too, especially if you are working from home. Make sure that there is nothing in the background that may cause offence to others such as religious texts or symbols, or calendars with pictures perhaps of people sunbathing or anything that could be distracting. If the background is plain, it can look rather bleak. Equally if all your coffee cups are waiting to be washed, it can distract from what you are saying. Some platforms allow you to choose a background. You could choose the setting of a beach or an exotic location, but be sensitive to the group you are training. Try to include some colour in the background. Some platforms allow you to blur your background so your image looks sharper. Others even allow you to improve how you look slightly, such as to eliminate your wrinkles!

If the participants can access the online training materials before they see you at the first live session, record and upload a short video of you introducing the course materials, so they can see what you look like from the start. Ask participants to upload their photograph too. Seeing what the other participants look like and interacting with them at live events, will increase your rapport and create a stronger bond within the group. But some may feel uncomfortable doing this for cultural or religious reasons and should not be pressured to do so.

See if the platform or your device's camera allows you to preview how you will appear, and adjust appropriately. It is good to show from your head as far down as the middle of your chest, so you fill a large part of the screen. Place the camera at about your eye level. If you can see a lot of ceiling on the screen, move the camera to see more of you. Many people do not like to see themselves on screen or hear the sound of their own voice, but participants will not care about this at all. Their focus is simply on getting what they need from you, and your focus should be on giving it – as long as you are able to communicate clearly with as few distractions or technical problems as possible, you can relax. Some platforms allow you to hide your 'self-view' so you do not need to look at yourself during the session.

Be kind

With face-to-face courses, participants will have spent time travelling to the training venue. In contrast, at a live online training session, everyone comes together at the click of a mouse, so probably are still thinking about whatever happened immediately before. It could be anything, sad or happy, for example hearing that a relative is seriously ill, or that their child has passed an exam. Participants may not have had time to process that, and it is good to encourage participants to build in a few minutes to transition, before they arrive online. Trainers need to be aware of this and treat everyone with respect and kindness. At the start of a live event, ask each participant to 'check-in' with the group, and say something about how they are feeling. This needs to be done sensitively, not forcing anyone to say anything they do not want to. If the training is for longer than one session, you could ask each participant in turn to identify something they have learned so far, or from the previous session. This helps participants to adjust back into the learning mode, and to fully participate in the session.

Cross-cultural training online

The training should have a structure and the same stated learning objectives as a face-to-face event, and follow a logical pattern to make it accessible and easy to follow. Online content needs to be at a high standard, while at the same time including variety so that participants with any preferred learning style can enjoy the experience. The trainer's inputs must be delivered with enthusiasm and fun to motivate everyone to learn. Online training can be a live session, where everyone is present on screen at the same time and can see and hear each other, for example in a 'webinar'. Or, it can be a part of longer training with self-contained learning materials online.

If the trainer has travelled from elsewhere, face-to-face training means they are absorbing the participant's culture from the moment they arrive and, even without knowing, start to adapt to that culture. In some situations, participants themselves may have travelled to a central venue and may represent a range of cultures. Online training makes it harder to replicate what it feels like in a different culture. Indeed, there is a danger that without actually travelling themselves, the trainer delivers content in a way that is more suitable to their own culture. One way to prompt cultural awareness is to ask the participants to 'give us a flavour of your culture' in an introductory activity. Ask each participant in advance to think about this and to perhaps bring a representative object of their culture to show on-screen, and describe its special meaning to the other participants.

In Chapter 3, we looked at the process of training from a cross-cultural perspective. We considered participatory training, and what happens at each stage of the learning process: *before the training starts, designing and preparing the content, delivering the training,* and *monitoring, evaluation, and learning after the training*. Most of these processes will equally apply whether the training is delivered face-to-face or online. However, there are some areas where online training provides new challenges, as well as new opportunities. We will look at these in turn:

Making 'online training courses' and 'blended learning' participatory

A participatory approach is one of the best ways of making any training accessible and appropriate for participants from different cultures. This is no less true for online training, which should be made as participatory as possible. The majority of the content should engage participants in 'doing' as well as 'seeing and listening'. Participants will need practical experience to learn new skills and behaviours.

For example, you could ask participants to investigate how their own organization monitors funded projects, discuss their findings with one other person in the group, and then report on what they have found in a live session. They could then receive additional feedback from the trainer and those in other groups.

Some tools that you can use as part of participatory online training are shown in Figure 5.1. Most of these tools are self-explanatory, but it is worth saying a little more about them.

Forums. Most learning platforms will have a place where participants can show the task they have completed, and leave their comments. Some will have an 'open' space which all the participants can see and add their comments. Often there will be a confidential space allowing individuals to upload their completed work. Trainers can see all of these comments, but can also send a private message to a participant. Trainers also need to monitor ongoing comments, and add their own thoughts to encourage and sometimes to gently correct any misunderstandings. A forum is a crucial part of online learning and it is important to encourage everyone to use it, but be aware that second language English speakers may feel less confident expressing their views in this way and may need extra help. Maybe the ground rules of the training will need to spell out what happens if a participant does not 'post' their thoughts and work. For example, they may be contacted by the trainer. However, be sensitive to cultural and personality reasons why participants may choose not to. In live events and for single training events, the 'chat' facility is often the equivalent of a forum.

Audio and video clips. These can be a powerful tool for online learning. There is however a wide variety in the quality of clips, so make sure they are from a reputable source and do not contradict anything you write in the other materials. Use the clips creatively, and always try to ask participants not to just

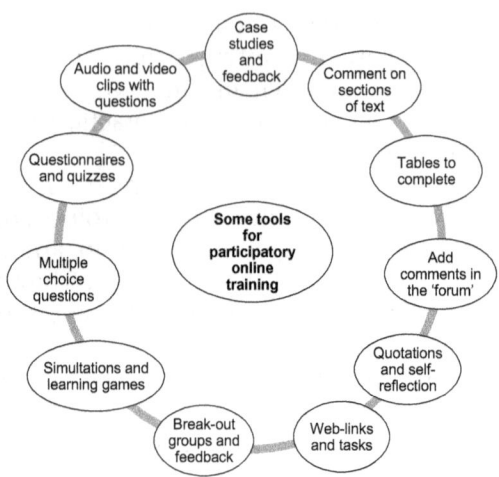

Figure 5.1 Some tools for participatory online training

watch them, but rather to pick out particular learning points and comment on them. You can usually find material by world experts in almost any topic, so take advantage of this.

You might also like to create your own audio and video clips. This gives variety to the materials and it is reassuring for participants to see the trainer as well as reading the materials. Often a clip of a minute or two can be enough to introduce a topic.

Break-out groups. As with face-to-face, use paired and group work to give everyone practical 'hands-on' experience, both at live events and when participants use the online materials. Try to divide the groups so that the same participants are not always together. For certain activities, it may be helpful to put together participants from the same first language group. As with a face-to-face course, the trainer moves around virtual groups at a live event to see how each group is getting on, and to offer further ideas. When it is time to return, simply 'click' to bring the groups back together and let each report on what they have found. Bringing groups back online is much more immediate than its face-to-face equivalent, so make sure you give at least a five-minute and two-minute warning!

Answers to activities. It is useful to prepare an answer sheet for activities whenever possible, especially if there is a unique solution. Most learning platforms have a facility for the answer to be seen only after the participant has attempted the activity. This assists all learning, but when working cross-culturally it can be a useful check on understanding and often a model for how a particular task should be approached and presented.

Add as much variety as you can to your materials. Include only one or two key messages on screen at any one time, especially at live events, and enhance each page with attractive backgrounds and colours. Resist the temptation to add too much text. Instead, break it up with graphics, pie charts, pictures, and links to other information. You could add appropriate quotations, and even cartoons and animations to keep participants' interest. Always check when using pictures, cartoons, audio and video clips and other graphics that they are free to use or, if copyrighted, ask for permission to use them for educational purposes. Make sure you show the source of any material used.

Keep checking how your materials will look from the viewpoint of participants from cultures other than your own. Refer to the material in Chapter 3 about delivering cross-cultural training, especially about giving instructions (Box 3.5, page 43), and asking and answering questions (Boxes 3.7 and 3.8, starting on page 53).

Be innovative and creative with your visual aids. If you are designing online training for the first time, look for ideas from professional information-giving websites, and see how television professionals present information visually. A general principle could be: if you can imagine it, you can do it! The limits are likely to be mostly technical, so work closely with a technical expert to see if and how what you want can be achieved.

For online training lasting for more than a week, the materials should be complemented with live sessions where the trainer can meet participants to discuss any issues they have, answer questions, and introduce new ideas. Trainers can also refer participants to further materials in printed books, e-books, and online. Some institutions offering training have libraries that offer online access to a range of different materials, including expensive books, and journal subscriptions that may also be useful.

In live sessions, whether for single events or longer training, make use of whatever tools your platform allows. Examples include:

- encouraging everyone to use the 'chat' facility to say hello, make comments, and ask questions;
- the trainer using 'chat' to write up any new or unusual words;
- clicking on a 'hand' icon to say you want add something (or typing 'hand' into the chat box);
- 'polling', for example, from six statements displayed, which one do participants think is the most frequent reason why organizations stop operating;
- drawing on the online whiteboard;
- clicking on a tick or a cross to agree or disagree with a question;
- clicking on an 'emoji' or 'reaction' though try to be aware in advance about the cultural acceptability of these, and of gestures, see page 86;
- sharing your screen with others;
- showing an online whiteboard to have a 'brainstorming' session, or to gather ideas;
- asking each participant for a suggestion about a particular topic, for example, 'let's think of types of donors who give money to non-profit organizations'.

Before the training starts

When English is a second-language

Online training can have distinct advantages for participants with English as a second language. Firstly, you can prepare the materials in advance, and participants can read them in advance and check the meaning of technical words ahead of the live session. For longer online training courses, provide an online glossary of terminology with the materials. If possible, translate terminology into the participant's first language. If there is time and resources available, all of the materials could be translated.

In addition, any pre-recorded audio and video clips should have a transcript available to download. This is also useful for those with a poor internet connection or issues of accessibility. If you put subtitles on pre-recorded video clips, it helps second-language English speakers to understand a new accent more easily. Any recordings can be reviewed a number of times. Say how long the clip lasts if not already shown in the software. Some platforms will aim to write on the screen what is spoken at live events, which can be helpful. Be aware though that the translation may not always be accurate! During live training events where the whole group gets together, a translator can sit with any participant to help clarify words that are not heard or understood.

Designing and preparing the content
Training plans and possible assessment

The design and preparation of online training takes more time than face-to-face sessions. Make sure there is sufficient variety of methods and activities included to keep participants fully engaged. Ask them to participate directly every four to five minutes, for example answering a poll question, writing on the white board, putting something in 'chat', being part of a discussion or joining a virtual 'breakout' group. For online training over several weeks, you could ask participants to present some work, either individually or jointly with others that might be assessed. It could be a single piece of work each week or, alternatively, be uploaded weekly to form part of the final assignment. It can encourage participants to apply what they learn to their workplace. This assessment could be a requirement of meeting the course learning objectives leading to the presentation of a certificate, or sometimes a formal qualification.

Delivering the training
'Live' events

All live events are a time when the trainer(s) and participants share time together on screen. For 'one-to-one' training, 'conference calls' and 'webinars' it is usually a single event. But for 'online training events' and 'blended learning', it may be a weekly session of one to two hours, as part of the self-study of learning materials and activities available through the chosen learning platform. The live session is a chance to raise questions, challenge participants, and relate the learning to real-life issues.

When planning the live session send people joining instructions with learning objectives and what you intend to include. This will prepare them in advance and help them to think of questions they want to ask. If participants are new to the platform give them instructions on how to use it, and encourage them, if possible, to try it out beforehand. Explain any participatory features of the particular platform, especially how to use 'chat' to talk to each other and ask questions. Explain how the 'mute/unmute' icon works and the etiquette of when to use either. Keeping the mute on unless you are speaking helps to exclude any disturbing background noise. On some platforms, the host has the power to stop people talking by muting everyone's or an individual's microphone. This is something trainers in face-to-face sessions might often like to do!

Be careful using gestures on screen with a group from diverse cultures. See the *Dos and don'ts in other cultures* in Chapter 2, starting on page 20. Any gesture you make will be magnified on screen. The 'thumbs up' gesture needs special care cross-culturally. It is used a lot online, to say you 'like' a posting, and it has become a non-verbal visual shorthand for saying 'I agree' or that you understand something. However, the sign is considered rude, particularly in the Middle East, parts of West Africa, and parts of Asia, as well as in Greece and Russia. Do not use it unless you know for sure that no one is likely to be offended. Find other visual ways to say 'well done'. Some platforms show clapping hands as a 'reaction'. Instead, if you are technically able (or you know someone who is) try showing a short video clip of a firework display, or of singers from one of the cultures represented singing a celebratory song, when something has gone well.

It is important to arrange the time for live events which means no one has to stay up too late, or get up too early. It is not always easy with international groups from different time zones, but worth considering. An alternative might be to repeat the event with better timings, for two smaller groups.

In an online group, you don't have all the usual clues of participants' engagement as you might in the training room. For example, if one of the participants was feeling sleepy, how would you notice? Try to pick up 'body language' signals by their involvement in discussions, whether they are contributing to chat and polls. But recognize this format could be new and they might be finding it challenging.

Arrival activities

For live online training, some arrival activities can be the same or similar to those in face-to-face training. When setting up an online session, it is useful to allow about 20 minutes before the start time for participants to log-in to the site and resolve any technical problems. If not, valuable session time will be used for this, frustrating both trainers and other participants. In addition, it is good to show a 'welcome' screen in the first language of those attending. For those who have not used the platform before it is useful to have some images and instructions of how to perform basic tasks, on a rolling screen during the 15 minutes before starting. You might also ask people to introduce themselves to the group during this time through 'chat' or something similar as they arrive. There can be a short arrival activity, interspersed with the introductions and instructions.

Culturally appropriate starts

Be aware of who is in the group, and of the material in Chapter 2 about 'high-' and 'low-context' cultures. In high-context cultures the group may expect a little general chat at the beginning to help everyone to relax. Those in low-context cultures may want to get straight down to business. In webinars that last an hour, for example, there is little opportunity to do anything other than start immediately. But in live sessions for courses lasting several weeks, it is worth investing a little time at the beginning of each session on more general talk. For those from a high-context background, they may feel more relaxed and learn more from the session.

Starting a training event

Sessions that last an hour or two, and live sessions require quite a lot of information at the start and it is easy for the trainer to miss something important. Some trainers find it is useful to make a checklist for themselves, and any other presenters, to leave less to chance and memory. An example is shown in Box 5.2. It is important to have an attention-grabbing start, so try to learn this off by heart, rehearse it and present it confidently. For the rest have rough headings and a list of points, to make sure you keep to time. It is sometimes helpful to imagine you are talking to just one or two participants, rather than to a camera.

Box 5.2 Example of a checklist for the trainer to start a 'live' event

1. Arrive in time to have a practice run through, if you have not done so already.
2. Make sure you are absolutely ready to start at least half an hour before the start time, with water for the presenters.
3. Open the platform ready for participants to join about 20 minutes before start time.
4. Make sure someone (or you!) is ready to help any participant with a technical problem.
5. Keep an eye on chat, respond to comments as needed, and add your welcome to everyone there.
6. A couple of minutes before the start time, verbally update everyone that you are about to start.
7. Start on time.
8. Welcome everyone again, with a 'smile' in your voice, thank them for being there, and deal with any housekeeping: for example, turning off phones/emails, not interrupting the person speaking.
9. Explain ways to ask questions and comment.
10. Tell the group if the session will be recorded, and when they will receive the link.
11. For a group of about 10 or fewer, ask everyone to say hello (introduce themselves if they do not already know each other), and say how their morning/afternoon/day has been so far. Call everyone by their name.
12. Outline the structure and start on the session's material.

Keeping people engaged at 'live' events

The secret is to include lots of variety to keep participants engaged with their learning. Find something different for them to look at or do every few minutes. Be friendly and approachable. Notice the clues in participants' reactions through their image, the tone of their voice if they speak, whether they are answering questions or are being distracted. When people comment in 'chat' or make a comment, thank them, referring to them by name. At live events as part of a longer training session with an established group, ask someone to keep time and remind everyone, including you, if going over the allocated time, maybe someone else could summarize the session. If people are looking tired and are not concentrating, have a break to make a drink. This can be useful trick too, if the technology goes wrong. It is good to give everyone permission to stand up and move around if they need to. A break every hour is certainly needed if concentrating on a screen.

Vary your voice too, in tone, pitch, pace and speed. Make sure your diction is as clear as possible. Try not to speak too quickly. Tell stories so that participants pay attention to them and remember the points you make more easily. Be enthusiastic about the topic.

Remember that everyone has a different learning style, so if someone is not reacting much it may be that they are writing notes and listening carefully to what you are saying. Some will join large online training groups because they do not want to be noticed. This can indicate that they really want to hear what you have to say.

Monitoring, evaluation, and learning after the training

Monitoring and evaluation

The ways for a trainer to monitor and evaluate learning are similar to any face-to-face training (see Chapter 3, starting on page 54). With a short online training session lasting an hour or two, it's worth encouraging participants to give you feedback, either verbally at the end of the session, or by encouraging them to complete an online questionnaire or post their comments in chat or social media. For online training lasting more than a week, ask for feedback as part of the learning materials each week. This will allow time to make changes, if possible, for this course, and improve the participants' experience now and in the future.

It is important to receive feedback about live sessions that support online training courses and 'blended' learning. If this happens each week it is important to discover what participants from different cultures think about the trainer's pace and whether the content is pitched at the right level. Ask especially how well they understand your English. Encourage participants to tell you honestly how they are finding the training.

Further learning

Organizing a follow-up session after the main training event has happened can add value to both face-to-face and online training. It might be a conversation a few weeks or months afterwards with individual participants as well as with the whole group. It could be offered as part of the original training package. It is perhaps more possible, and cost-effective, when everything has been online, to consolidate and build on the relationship that trainers and participants have developed.

See Chapter 9, starting on page 180 *Frequently asked questions about online learning.*

CHAPTER 6
Cross-cultural financial training

This chapter looks at specific challenges for delivering financial training, and what type of training different people need throughout an organization. It includes a list of international document names, financial terms, and numbering systems. It ends with some practical tips about delivering financial training.

Keywords: financial training, fear of finance, participatory financial training, international finance documents, international finance terms, finance training tips

> *We can live as brothers and sisters but straight accounting should be between us (Pashto proverb).*

We have been looking at training in general. However, there are particular challenges to consider when planning and delivering *financial* training, which is why it requires this additional chapter. This is partly due to the technical aspects of finance and partly due to many people's fear of numbers. This chapter will show how to help participants engage with finance in a positive and accessible way, overcoming these fears.

Specific challenges with finance training

Challenges include:
- Assessing whether 'training' is the answer to the needs.
- Finding trainers who understand finance, and also know how to train.
- Deciding which staff to invite to training events and what content to include.
- Making finance training participatory and accessible for everybody.

http://dx.doi.org/10.3362/9781788531085.006

Responding to these challenges

Is training the answer?

When people are sent to a training event, it is assumed that they need to change in some way – perhaps to change their behaviour, or the level of their skills. Hopefully, a 'training needs analysis' (see pages 26–27) has identified what the change should be, but this does not always happen.

For example, someone has signed up for a training event to help them interpret financial reports that they receive as part of their job. When a trainer talks with them, they find that the person is highly intelligent, but they just cannot understand the monthly report. As a result, they have concluded that they have not had enough training. When the trainer looks at the report the participant has brought along, they can see that it is poorly designed and confusing. Training may help a little, but the problem really demands that the organization redesigns its report in a user-friendly way. The finance staff may need training instead, about how to communicate this information in a way that can be understood by non-finance people. Box 6.1 provides questions for an organization to ask itself before it decides whether it needs financial training.

Finding Trainers

When a 'training needs assessment' has been completed and a decision has been made to organize some finance training, the first decision is who should lead it. If the training is for an individual or a group, then ask:

- Do we have someone in our organization to deliver the training?
- Can we afford an external trainer to deliver this training 'in-house'? Either face-to-face or electronically.
- Is in-house training something we could share with our partners or other organizations?
- If not, can we send our staff to an external training course?

Sometimes large organizations use one of their finance team who is experienced in delivering training in a participatory way. Smaller organizations can find this more difficult

Box 6.1 Deciding whether to use a training event to build financial management capacity

Green – go ahead if:
- you have fully assessed the training needs;
- the training is part of other capacity-building initiatives;
- the members of the group have similar backgrounds and experience;
- it will increase the profile of finance within the organization;
- it will encourage senior managers and management committees to develop their financial management skills;
- it will encourage non-finance people to use financial management skills;
- it will develop the skills of finance staff.

Amber – be careful if:
- you have not first considered other approaches to financial management capacity building;
- the training is not relevant to the needs of the participants;
- the facilitator is not able to use participatory training methods.

Red – do not proceed if:
- you think training will solve all your problems;
- you expect that it will simply make people do what you want them to;
- other approaches to financial management capacity building will work better.

Source: Based on an extract from Cammack, 2014

and often recruit an external trainer to deliver the training. The external trainer needs an understanding of the sector involved – for example if they are a trainer in the commercial sector, they may not understand the non-profit sector. If it is an 'in-house' training course, it is helpful to have some of the finance team there as well, to answer internal questions and to build their own relationships with participants. The trainer should recognize when finance staff themselves are the best people to lead a session.

A training event can be an opportunity to share common knowledge and concerns. It can also encourage finance and other teams to cooperate more closely for the benefit of the organization, and other partner organizations with which they are involved.

Who to train and what to include?

A wide range of people can benefit from finance training. Ideally, it will be based on a training needs analysis (see Chapter 3, starting on page 26) and planned around it. However, there are specific types of training that are suitable for those with different reasons for understanding finance (based on Cammack, 2012):

Induction training. New staff usually need training in finance and financial management systems and procedures. This can cover, for example, claiming expenses, completing monthly documents, and ordering and approving expenditure. Ideally, this training will take place when the new staff have got used to the organization and know the questions they need to ask. In addition, they will sometimes need a one-to-one session with a finance person soon after they arrive to look at tasks they need to do immediately.

Financial management for non-financial managers. Managers are likely to need input on topics such as what financial management is, preparing budgets and cash flow, interpreting financial information, internal financial controls, and managing audits. They may also need sessions on how to write reports for donors, and on more specific accounting and financial management tasks.

Financial management for senior managers. Senior managers need everything listed for non-financial managers above, but also the skills involved for strategic financial management. These include managing reserves, funding administrative costs, and creating a sustainable financial management strategy. They may also need input on developing finance and management controls, and how to monitor these effectively as a director. Senior managers also need to understand the importance of the strong relationship between finance and non-finance colleagues.

Senior managers who struggle to understand their financial management role can be reluctant to attend a training course for fear of losing face. If they have been responsible for approving financial documents for some time, it can be hard to admit that they do not fully understand the task, especially in some cultures. At worst their lack of skills can mean that donors lose confidence in their organization. Confidential tutoring is where an outside tutor can have a number of private sessions with the staff member. This can provide the training needed without them losing face. The tutor could possibly then act as the staff member's ongoing mentor.

Financial management for management committee members. Management committee members (trustees) are usually busy people and not often available to attend long training events. It is important to make sure you design material to fit their available time, prioritizing what is most important for their specific needs. It is sometimes possible to contribute to one of the management committee's regular meetings. Members are likely to need help with strategic financial management, how to interpret budgets and other financial reports, and how to identify their own financial responsibilities.

Training for finance staff. All of the topics listed above, possibly with a different emphasis. Training and learning in technical accounting usually comes from outside the organization, and it is worth checking what is available locally. Medium to large organizations will also need professionally qualified accountants. A number of routes to this qualification are offered by professional accounting bodies in different parts of the world. The question for organizations is often whether they will financially support their staff to obtain the qualification. The alternative is often to 'buy in' staff that qualified elsewhere.

Communicating about finance for finance and non-finance staff. It is crucial that finance staff and managers and other non-finance staff can communicate with each other. Specialist communication courses are available, and ideally need to be specifically for finance people working, for example, with non-finance colleagues in a different department.

Sector-specific training. Recently appointed finance and other staff who are working in a new organization, or even a new sector, for the first time may need something in addition to their induction training. The culture they experience can feel unfamiliar, and it is important for everyone that they feel comfortable in it as soon as possible. It is essential that finance staff quickly become familiar with the priorities of the organization.

Training finance trainers. People with financial skills do not always have the skills to train others. It is important therefore to identify staff with potential for this, and invest in their training. This skill is valuable both within an organization and when working with its partner groups. Courses are especially useful if they show how to train with a participatory approach which allows their training to be practically based.

Participatory finance training

In all training, an interactive participatory approach (see Chapter 3) is most likely to achieve the best training outcomes. This is certainly the case with finance training. A lot of the tasks that need to be completed in finance work can only be achieved by allowing a 'hands-on' experience.

For course design, this means making sure you have enough activities that can be used throughout the training. For in-house courses, try to use materials which are laid out in that organization's format to make sure the learning is grounded in what the participants need to know. Sometimes training events have computers for each learner, especially if learning about a particular accounting or spreadsheet package. At other times participants will be working with pen and paper, and need paper copies of the activity. This can be preferable as it is easier to make sure everyone is learning at the same pace. For all activities that have a unique solution, it is good to print off copies to give to participants.

Another effective technique is to use storytelling to help bring financial issues to life. This is especially useful as part of cross-cultural financial training. Ask participants to share their stories about, for example, experiences of being audited, poor communication about financial information, or how budgets helped or hindered a project. It is also worth encouraging participants to 'tell a story about the figures'. Ask them to interpret figures and explain what might be happening in the programme or department concerned. If this is a real situation, you may be able to reveal what actually was happening. This is a great way to encourage a group to understand more about what lies 'behind' the figures and widen their understanding of the information in a creative way.

Participants feel threatened

Some participants feel more nervous about attending a finance course than a course for any other subject. It can remind them of school maths lessons, and any feeling of inadequacy that they still have from them. This is a challenge for the trainer who has to work hard to gain their trust. They need to make sure that they create a friendly and 'safe' environment where no participant is criticized or made to lose face or look foolish when they get things wrong. It is good to explain at the start of the training that although there is some maths involved in finance, most of it is about techniques of interpreting information. Say that you will go through each activity step-by-step to make sure everyone fully understands. One of the most rewarding parts of finance training is having someone who was terrified when they arrived leave thinking it can actually be fun to prepare a budget!

Relating the content to what participants already know

You can help reassure participants by using financial reports that are familiar to them. If you are working with one organization you can use its own reports, even if the participants do not quite understand them yet. Part of the task will be to show them why the report is important, what it means, and allow time to practise interpreting it. Even when the report's format is familiar, make sure you explain it in detail. Allow time for questions.

When working internationally, make sure the examples you use are in the currency of the country you are in. Use the same title for a document that people in that country or organization use. For example, if they call it 'a budget and actual report' use that title and do not call it 'management accounts'. The meaning is the same, but it makes learning much easier.

If some of the technical words are not familiar, explain what they mean. A good way to do this is to ask participants 'do you know what is meant by "cash flow forecast"?' Someone may say they do and, if so, ask them to explain to the others. If not, explain yourself, drawing out the similarities to what the participants already know.

Participants' experience in their everyday lives can be useful for learning. Many will have a personal bank account, and know how it operates. Others will pay bills regularly and understand the consequences of late payment. Some will have bank or credit cards. Use this experience as the basis to explain what happens in an organization. If talking about cash flow forecasts, ask how participants manage their personal finances to make sure they have enough money to pay all their bills.

International document names, financial terms and numbering systems

Differences in document names and terminology

Accounting and financial management terms and systems are remarkably similar throughout the world. However, documents are presented differently, and other words can be used to mean the same. Some alternative names for financial documents used internationally are shown in Table 6.1.

Write handouts in plain English and explain all technical terms. If the group contains people from a number of countries, ask participants what they call a particular item. Table 6.2 shows a number of alternative financial terms which are used internationally with the same meaning.

Many non-finance participants will be especially worried by finance terminology, so it is worth spending time on this during the training. Avoid using technical terms, as much as possible, unless you are absolutely sure everyone in the group understands them. Participants from some cultures may use completely different words from the ones you use. If in doubt ask: 'what do you call it when…?' If you do use technical terms, make sure you explain what they mean first, before saying 'the technical term for this is…'. The 'terminology quiz' shown in Chapter 11, 'Energizing activities', will consolidate the learning about terminology and increase participants' confidence to use it.

Numbering systems

There are a variety of ways of writing numbers across different countries. Use whatever system is most familiar for participants.

Table 6.1 Alternative names for financial documents used internationally

Term	Alternatives terms for the same document
Balance sheet	Liabilities and owners' equity, position statement, statement of affairs, statement of assets, statement of assets and liabilities, statement of condition, statement of financial position
Cash and bank book	Cash book, cash receipts and payments journal, daybook
Income statement	Account of operations, income and disbursements account, income and expenditure account, operating statement, revenue account, revenue statement, statement of earnings, statement of expenditure and revenues, statement of income and expenditure, statement of profit and loss
Management accounts	Budget and actual report, budget report, financial report, monthly figures, variances, variance reports
Profit and loss account	Earnings statement, operating statement, p and l, profit and loss statement, revenue statement, statement of financial performance, statement of operations

Table 6.2 Alternative names for financial terms used internationally

Term	Alternative term
Deficit	Excess of expenditure over income, loss
Employees saving scheme	Thrift fund, thrift savings plan, pension fund
Expenditure	Expenses
Fixed assets	Long lived assets, permanent assets
Furniture, computers	Mobile assets
Income	Revenue
Inventory	List of what we own, stock held
Land and buildings	Immobile assets
Liabilities	Things we owe
Local travel	Conveyance
Net profit	Net margin
Pension fund	Provident fund
Prepayments	Payments in advance
Restricted funds	Earmarked funds, ring-fenced funds, tied funds
Sales	Revenue, turnover
Stock	Inventories, inventory
Surplus	Excess of income over expenditure, profit
Unrestricted funds	General purposes income, free money

This will be appreciated and will give the trainer credibility. Some examples are:

South Asia numbers

In South Asia, numbers have the comma before every two zeros, after the first thousand. Therefore, a *lakh* (or lac), one hundred thousand, is written as 1,00,000; 10 lakhs, a million, is written 10,00,000; and a *crore*, 10 million, is written 1,00,00,000. One hundred crore, 1 billion (sometimes called an *arab*), is written 1,00,00,00,000.

Arabic numbers

People in most Arabic speaking countries either use, or at least recognize Western numerals. However, there are some countries, mostly in the Middle East and North Africa, that also use Arabic numeric characters. These numbers, unlike Arabic words, are printed from left to right. They are shown in Table 6.3.

Other scripts

Other countries, for example China and Thailand, have their own script for writing numbers. However, if the training is in English, it is likely that participants will expect to use, and be familiar with, Western numerals. If in doubt, check with your local contact about what is appropriate.

Finance training for non-literate groups

In the international non-profit sector, it is sometimes necessary to train those who cannot read or write confidently, in financial skills. Delivering this training gives you an opportunity to look at the content of the training materials and judge how clearly they are presented. You could try changing the format and replacing words with pictures, diagrams, verbal and visual activities, and objects to give the quantity and value that you want to show participants. Sometimes it is essential to have things written down. In that case, you could use a system of

Table 6.3 Arabic and Western numbers

Western number	Arabic number	Arabic word	Western number	Arabic number	Arabic word
1	١	waaHid	11	١١	iH'dash or H'dash
2	٢	tinain or ithnain	12	١٢	it'nash or t'nash
3	٣	talaata or thalaatha	13	١٣	talaatash
4	٤	arba'a	14	١٤	arba'tash
5	٥	khamseh	15	١٥	khamistash
6	٦	sitah	16	١٦	sittash
7	٧	saba'a	17	١٧	saba'tash
8	٨	thamaaniyeh or tamaaniyeh	18	١٨	tamaantash
9	٩	tisa'a	19	١٩	tisatash
10	١٠	asharah	20	٢٠	ashriin

boxes to represent the type of income or expenditure, and marks in the boxes to represent how much money has been received and spent. Participants may need to use written financial information as part of their role. If so, you could ask participants if they would like to invite a literate relative or friend to work with them and accompany them to the training.

Tips when delivering finance training

- Provide practical tools that participants can use immediately when they return to their workplace.
- Begin the training with an activity that does not include figures.
- Start with the basics of each topic before moving on to more complex areas.
- Build on what participants know about finance already, for example personal bank accounts, personal budgeting, and cash management.
- Do not show lots of figures when training non-finance people. Instead, build up gradually and show a few figures, explaining what they mean.
- Keep building on what the participants have already seen and understood.

- Highlight the most important figures and what they mean.
- Show any 'accountants' abbreviations in full for example 'year to date' instead of 'ytd', 'last year' rather than 'ly'.
- If you are using an organization's own documents which include abbreviations, explain what they mean as soon as the copies are circulated to participants.
- Explain the meaning before using a technical accounting term.
- Remove any non-essential figures, words, or information from the activities.
- When showing the group an activity involving numbers and calculations, make sure you have tested it out on your own beforehand.
- Make the documents you use appropriate for the group you are working with. Show examples that they are likely to see in their everyday work.
- Use currencies that the group use themselves. If participants are from different countries, use different currencies in case studies and activities, and when giving examples yourself.
- Make sure any place names or other references, such as in case studies, are relevant to where the participants live and work.
- Let participants have hands-on experience.
- Prepare an attractive handbook to accompany the training.
- Include a glossary of financial terms.
- Have calculators available.
- Use a variety of training methods to keep things fresh – invent your own methods.
- Have fun!

More tips about delivering financial training and explaining financial terms simply are shown in *Communicating financial management with non-finance people' (Cammack, 2012)*.

CHAPTER 7

Training in specific countries

Training in any country or culture needs careful preparation. The 10 country sections in this chapter give guidance on how to train in those cultures, and goes through questions that should be asked about any new culture. The chapter provides general guidance for all cultures, and concludes with practical tips you can adopt when travelling.

Keywords: cultural greetings, conversation topics, trainer's dress code, gender and equality, travel practicalities, public holidays, travelling

The aim of this chapter is to give some more detailed examples. Certainly, the country sections will be particularly helpful if you are delivering face-to-face training there, or if your online participants are from there. Wherever you are, these examples can introduce you to the kinds of cultural questions to ask and find answers to, before and during your training.

It is worth remembering that although you may facilitate a training event in one of these countries, the participants can be drawn from a range of other countries and cultures.

In the following country sections there are some phrases in the most frequently spoken language but do not assume that it is the only language spoken there. Find out the best language to use with the participants. The words shown for each country are just intended as a starting point. Participants will really appreciate you using a few words from their own language.

Check how to pronounce the words with colleagues and participants. Sometimes the spelling in this text is based is based on translating them into English to help pronunciation. A number of different spellings can be used.

The fact files give basic information about the country. The population and land areas are from Worldometers.info and populations of other countries and cities can be found there.

http://dx.doi.org/10.3362/9781788531085.007

Each of the country sections covers the same topics, which are:
- Greetings
- Words of greeting
- Business cards
- Course certificates
- Names
- Gender and equality
- Language
- Dress for the trainer
- Working week and holidays
- Culture and time
- Building rapport
- Conversation topics
- Training tips

Training in Bangladesh

The face is the index of the mind (Bengali proverb).

Greetings

With the same gender, greetings are by shaking hands. If greeting a member of the opposite sex, wait for the other person to offer their hand to you. If a hand is not offered, just nod and smile. Hugs and kisses are not usually exchanged, although this sometimes happens with the same gender. Show respect to more senior and older people, and introduce them first. For Hindus in Bangladesh, put your hands together just below your chin and close to your body, and nod your head slightly.

Words of greeting

In villages and outside the main cities *Assalamu aliakum* (peace be upon you) is common among Muslims. The response is *Walaikum assalam* (peace be upon you too). If this is not used just say 'hello'. In West Bengal, or if working with Hindus, use *Namashkar*.

Business cards

Cards are exchanged at an initial meeting. Educational qualifications will be especially valued so include them on your card, with your current job title. Present and receive the card with your

Box 7.1 Fact file: Bangladesh

Full name	People's Republic of Bangladesh
Capital	Dhaka
National population	164,689,383 (Dhaka: 10,356,500)
Land area	130,170 square kilometres
Main language(s)	Bengali or Bangla (official). English. Sometimes Urdu is spoken in cities
Predominant religion	Muslim (89%), Hindu (10%)
Currency	Bangladeshi Taka (Tk or BDT) divided into 100 paisha
Time	GMT + 6 hours
Telephone code	+ 880

right hand. When receiving a card, look at it carefully before putting it away, and possibly ask a question about it. If you have a Bangladeshi telephone number, write this on your card.

Course certificates

Present certificates with the right hand.

Names

A first name will often be *Mohammed* (or *Md*) for a man, and *Mosammot* (or *Mst*) for a woman. The 'given name' that a participant wishes to be called by, usually follows *Mohammed* or *Mosammot*. The last names will often be another name for God, for example *Rahman*. In training events, ask participants what they want to be called and let them write their name on a name card or badge. Only use someone's given name after they use yours. Using someone's given name is more accepted if the person is younger than you, or if they are a friend.

People of about the same age, or a little older, can be called by their given name with *Bhai* (brother) or *Apa* (sister) after it. This shows affection and trust for the person. For an older person, *Chacha* (uncle) can be added after his given name, or *Khala* (aunty) after her given name. However, be careful not to make assumptions about someone's age. When introducing someone formally, you could use *Mr* and *Ms* before their given name to show respect.

Gender and equality

Gender discrimination continues to be a concern in Bangladesh. Women might not be as forthcoming as men in training events. Make sure you use techniques so that everyone can participate equally. Touching the body is usually not acceptable across the sexes, and should be avoided when planning training games or activities.

Language

English is often spoken in cities, and by professional people. Translators are likely to be needed if the training is in a rural area, or with people from a rural area who are attending in the city.
Some words in Bangla:

> Hello – *Assalamu aliakum* (Muslim), *Namashkar* (Hindu)
> Welcome – *Sāgatama*
> How are you? – *Kêmon achhen?* (The reply is *bhalo achi* meaning 'I am well')
> Thank you – *Dhonnobad*
> Goodbye – *Bhalo thakben*
> Good/fine – *Accha*
> Well done – *Sabas* or *Bhāla kāja*

Dress for the trainer

The aim is to dress modestly, so avoid sleeveless shirts, shorts, or short dresses. Dress smartly but casually. Women can wear trousers. If training with government officials, you will need more formal dress such as a jacket, or suit. Loose clothing should always be worn because of the heat.

Working week and holidays

The working week starts on Sunday and ends on Thursday evening, with Friday as a rest/prayer day. Saturday is also a rest day for many, although some offices remain open on Saturday.
Key dates to avoid include:

> 21 February – International Mother's Language Day
> 17 March – Bangabandhu's Birthday (Father of the Nation)
> 26 March – Independence Day

14 April – Bengali New Year's Day
1 May – Labour Day
15 August – National Mourning Day of the Father of the Nation
16 December – Victory Day
25 December – Christmas Day

Dates vary

The timing of the fasting month of *Ramadan* varies each year and follows the lunar cycle. It is best to avoid organizing training activities during this period of fasting, as participants are likely to be tired. It also seems insensitive if non-Muslim participants are eating while Muslim participants are not. Ramadan is followed by *Eid-ul-Fitr* (also known as the 'small Eid') and is a three-day public holiday. *Eid-ul-Ahza* (the 'second Eid') is also celebrated two and a half months after the Eid-ul-Fitr. This is also a three-day public holiday.

In addition, there are other public holidays – *Buddha Purnima, Sab-e-Barat, Sab-e-Qadar, Shuvo Janmashtami, Durga Puja, Ashura,* and *Eid-e-Milad-un-Nabi* – which also follow the lunar cycle. Check the exact dates with your local contact or the government official calendar.

Culture and time

There is a relaxed attitude to time, but Bangladeshis are usually on time for formal business meetings.

Building rapport

Bangladeshis have an open and welcoming attitude towards foreigners. Trust is built by being open and transparent, about yourself and what will happen in the work situation. Forming good personal relationships is important, and will make things happen more smoothly.

Conversation topics

Conversation traditionally starts by asking how you are and what you are doing. Sometimes questions can be direct, for example about your age, your salary, and whether you are married and have children. Most subjects are acceptable, but be careful not to express strong opinions especially if talking about politics and religion. People particularly like to talk about cricket, and with younger people, football, and also about food and culture.

Training tips

- Singing is sometimes used as an energizer. Ask one of the Bangladeshi participants to lead.
- If you do not know the answer to a question, it is all right to say 'I do not know but I will find out' (but make sure you do). If you do this too often, however, it can undermine your credibility.
- Do not lose your temper. This would lead to a loss of face and it would be difficult to maintain your dignity or to command respect afterwards.
- Make sure you show respect if someone answers a question incorrectly. Rather than saying 'no' or 'that's the wrong answer', say something like 'that might be possible but another way is to …'.
- Although many people will speak English, the level of understanding varies. Make sure you speak more clearly and slightly slower than you would usually.
- Facial gestures need to be controlled or even avoided as these can easily be misinterpreted (remember 'the face is the index of the mind').
- Do not show, or expect, too much eye contact. Bangladeshi women especially will often be embarrassed by this.
- For in-house courses, you might find the senior person answers your questions. Make sure you use lots of group work so that everyone has a chance to contribute.
- Bangladeshis will enjoy interactive and participatory sessions, so use a variety of methodologies, including group work, case studies, learning games, and discussions.

Training in Cambodia

> *You can know a lot, but respect other's knowledge (Khmer proverb).*

Box 7.2 Fact file: Cambodia

Full name	Kingdom of Cambodia
Capital	Phnom Penh
National population	16,718,965 (Phnom Penh: 1,573,544)
Land area	176,520 square kilometres
Main language(s)	Khmer (official), English and French widely spoken
Predominant religion	Theravada Buddhist (95%)
Currency	Cambodian riel (for KHR). The minimum note is 100 riels. The US dollar is widely used as a currency.
Time	GMT + 7 hours
Telephone code	+ 855

Greetings

The national greeting is to bow, bringing your hands together at about chest height. It is called the *som pbeah*. To signal greater respect, due to age or status, Cambodians will bow lower and lift the hands higher. When greeting foreigners, a (not too firm) hand shake is likely from men, although women will often give the traditional greeting. Otherwise wait for women to offer a hand. It is good practice to respond with the greeting you are offered. Sometimes Cambodians will place their left hand on their right elbow as they offer you a hand to shake, or a gift. Respect is always given to the most senior person. If you introduce others, you would be expected to always introduce the most senior person first.

Words of greeting

The words *chum reap sour* accompany the bow. When leaving the *som pbeah* is done again and the words of leaving are *chum reap lear*.

Business cards

Give your business card after the initial introductions, presenting it with both hands and, especially with a more senior person, a slight bow. Receive cards in the same way. Take interest in it and put it away carefully. Cambodians may think that how you treat the card is how you will treat the person.

Course certificates

Present certificates with both hands.

Names

It is usual for the family name to be used first and the given name second. The family name can be the father's family name, or another given name. Women usually keep their own name after marriage. When speaking, men's given names are often preceded by *Lok* and women's given names by *Lok srey*. Often when speaking, as a way of showing respect, instead of the actual name, Cambodians use:

> *Bong* – for a man of same age or a little older, similar to 'brother'.
> *Bong srey* – for a woman of same age or a little older, similar to 'sister'.
> *Pu* – for a man who is older, but younger than one's father. When older than one's father it is *Om*, similar to 'uncle'.
> *Ming* – for a woman who is older, but younger than one's mother. When older than one's mother it becomes *Om Srey,* similar to 'aunty'.

Gender and equality

Avoid physical contact in training sessions, especially between men and women. If you ask participants to hold hands for example, they will do so but only reluctantly. In large mixed gender groups, women might not feel comfortable speaking. Try to encourage everyone to report back after group work, at different stages of the training.

Language

Khmer is the official language, and English is spoken by professional and younger people. French is still spoken, but perhaps more by older people.

Some words in Khmer:

Hello – *Chum reap sour*
Welcome – *Svarkum* or *Saum Svarkum* are both formal welcomes to a meeting.
How are you? – *Sok sabay te* (said with an upward inflection as a question). Sometimes shortened to *sok sabay* (with inflection). Sometimes preceded by *bong, bong srey* or the equivalent. The reply is *sok sabay* ('I'm well').
Thank you – *Aw kun*, with the reply *men ei te* ('you are welcome').
Goodbye – *Chum reap lear*
Good/fine – *La'aw*
Well done – *La'aw nas*, or *Sa'thouk* ('how wonderful').

Dress for the trainer

Modest and respectful dress is required for trainers. When working with higher status people, and in government circles, dress should be more formal. When working with communities and non-profit organizations, smart casual dress is more usual. It is not appropriate to wear shorts when training, and doing so can lessen your credibility.

Working week and holidays

The working week is mostly from Monday to Friday, and hours are from 8 a.m. to 12 noon and 2 p.m. to 5.30 p.m. However, government offices, among others, tend to open and close a little earlier.

Key dates to avoid include:

1 January – International New Year's Day
7 January – Victory over the Genocidal Regime Day
13 or 14 April – Khmer New Year (*Chaul Chhnam*) lasting for three days
13, 14, 15 May – King's Birthday (*Norodom Sihamoni*)
19, 20, 21 September – *Pchum Ben* holiday
2, 3, 4 November – Water Festival (*Bon Om Touk*)

Cambodians can take the whole week as holiday for three-day festivals.

Culture and time

People are mostly on time for business meetings, especially in towns and cities. There is an expression for non-Westerners in Cambodia: 'time is timeless'. Therefore for participants to be late or not to show up at all is not considered to be too serious. However, trainers are still expected to be on time.

Building rapport

Rapport is built by getting to know the other person. Allow time to do this with Cambodian colleagues before the course starts. Aim to have had a conversation with all the training participants by the end of the first day.

Participants will want to know what experience you have that makes you suitable for the training. If possible, ask someone from the organization you are with to introduce you and talk about your background. This is especially helpful if you are a young, or young looking, trainer as it gives you more credibility. If you have not got a lot of experience in the subject, for example, stress that you *are* an experienced trainer.

Conversation topics

Be careful about talking about the Khmer Rouge administration or any other political regimes. Many people want to forget the atrocities that took place. Wait for others to raise the subject. Khmer culture is about respect, and being loyal to the authorities, and therefore avoiding any criticism.

Show interest in the participants' family and community. In the morning, ask 'how are you?' and a common question is 'have you had breakfast?' Some Cambodians ask foreigners personal questions to help identify the seniority of the person they are talking with. If asked how much you earn, you may want to find a way to avoid this question by talking about where you fit into your organization. Other Cambodians do not ask such questions to avoid embarrassment, but would still be interested in the answer.

Training tips

- Try not to be negative or critical in training sessions (even of yourself) as this can result in loss of face. Always be positive and encouraging.

- Remember that you need to show a respectful, gentle, and sensitive approach with participants. Smile and show humility.
- Make sure your posture shows respect. Lower your body when walking in front of an older or more senior person. Do not put your hands in your pockets. Do not put your hands on your hips, as this indicates impatience and arrogance. Do not put your feet on the desk or table or rest them on the chair.
- Showing emotions is not considered acceptable. This could result in loss of face. Instead try to adopt a calmer approach.
- Talk slowly and repeat any instructions several times.
- Cambodians are likely to tell you what they think you want to hear. This is considered polite. If you ask 'is that all right?' the answer will usually be 'yes'. Therefore ask 'open' rather than 'closed' questions. Try to phrase questions in a way that allows course participants to express a genuine lack of understanding without embarrassment.
- A participant may feel shame when called upon to answer a question in front of a group, if they do not know the answer.
- Education and training in Cambodia are often given in a 'talk and chalk' style, with little interaction with learners. Therefore, participatory approaches can be new to a group. Be confident that this approach works, but some participants can take a little while to become familiar with it.
- It is not unusual to find people talking and giggling to each other in the group. This is sometimes to translate and explain what you are saying.

Training in Ethiopia

When you criticize tell them privately, when you appreciate do it publicly (Ethiopian proverb).

Ethiopia is a large country with a number of distinct areas, cultures, languages, and dialects. These include Amhara, Oromia, Somali, and Tigray, but there are a large number of smaller ethnic groups, some of which are grouped in the Southern Nations, Nationalities and Peoples' Region (SNNPR). There are Christians and Muslims in most areas.

114 CROSS-CULTURAL ORGANIZATIONAL AND FINANCIAL TRAINING

Box 7.3 Fact file: Ethiopia

Full name	Federal Democratic Republic of Ethiopia (FDRE)
Capital	Addis Ababa
National population	114,963,588 (Addis Ababa: 2,757,729)
Land area	1,000,000 square kilometres
Main language(s)	Amharic (Amharigna) (working language for federal government), English (most widely used foreign language). Most professional people speak English. If training outside the main cities, check which language is used most. Other languages: Arabic, Guaragigna, Oromigna, Somali, and Tigrinya.
Predominant religion	Ethiopian Orthodox Christian and Muslim. Protestant Christians are a significant minority, especially in the southern states.
Currency	Ethiopian birr (Br or ETB) divided into 100 santim (cents). US dollars are sometimes accepted in Addis Ababa.
Time	GMT + 3 hours
Telephone code	+ 251

Greetings

A traditional welcome is a handshake while looking the person in the eye. For those with a strong personal or working relationship, a hug and three kisses. Men should wait for a Muslim woman to offer a hand. Older people should always be greeted first. Sometimes older people can receive a small bow especially in rural areas outside the cities. Usually the greeting will be followed by enquiring after each other's and their family's health – sometimes by asking 'are you fine?' And 'is your family fine?' This requires the answer that 'I am fine/well' or 'my family is fine/well'. Also, you might ask about the other person's work and life. These formalities should be given time and will take place as people gather.

Words of greeting

A formal greeting is *Tena yistillign* (may God give you health on my behalf). A more informal (and easier to remember) one is *Tadiyass* (hi, how are you?) which is often used by young people. For Muslims the international greeting of *Assalamu alaikum* (peace be upon you) is acceptable. At the start of a course/day, *Selam* (peace) is a suitable greeting for Christians and Muslims. For a little variety you might try: *Endemen aderachu* (good morning) and *Endemen arefedachehu* (good afternoon).

Business cards

Business cards are often used upon meeting. Present cards with the right hand. In traditional areas, to show more respect to older people, present with both hands together.

Course certificates

Present certificates with your right hand.

Names

Ethiopians are usually given a 'known-by' name at birth. They also add their father's first name, and possibly their grandfather's name as well. Not all members of the family have the same second or third name (although brothers and sisters do). The second and third names are not family names as in some other countries. Women therefore do not change their name when they are married. It is sometimes difficult from the name to know that people are married. Often you will be addressed by your title and your first name which gives respect. Amharic titles can be used: *Ato* (Mr), *Woizero* (Mrs), *Woizerit* (Miss), or Doctor. Equivalent titles are used for other ethnic groups. Always ask participants by which name they would like to be called.

Gender and equality

In cities and with professional participants, there are few taboos. But when using training activities with Muslim men and women, do not use anything that requires participants to touch those of the other sex. In more rural/traditional communities, men and women are often separated into two separate groups. Therefore, think carefully how to best facilitate the training, and who should lead it. There are usually more men in training events, and they can be more vocal than women. Make sure therefore that you give women every opportunity to participate and speak.

Language

The words used here are in the Amharic language but if training in other ethnic areas, try to find the equivalent.
Some words in Amharic (Amharigna):

> Hello – *Tenayistillign*, or *Tadiyass* (informal). The greeting *Selam* (peace) is used widely.
> Welcome – *Enkuan Dehina Metachu*
> How are you? – *Tadiyass* can also mean 'how are you' but also *Dehnaneh* (male), *Dehnanesh* (female), *Endimin allachu* (plural). The response is always *Dehena* (pronounced *dena*) meaning 'I am fine'.
> Thank you (very much) – *(Betam) Amesegenalehu*
> Goodbye – *Dehena hunu* or the informal Italian *Ciao*.
> Good/fine – *Tiru*
> Well done – *Bedenb Tekenawnoal*

Dress for the trainer

Dress modestly. Smart casual dress is usually appropriate, but smarter dress, for example, a jacket or suit, is required with senior and government officials. In Muslim areas, it may be preferable for women to wear long skirts but check with your local contact. Men should wear trousers rather than shorts when delivering training.

Working week and holidays

Normal office working hours are 8.30 a.m. to 12.30 p.m., and then 1.30 to 5.00 or 5.30 p.m. Monday to Friday. Some offices and banks work from 8.30 to 11.00 a.m. on Saturday. Training days are likely to be similar. Training is not usually undertaken on Saturdays and Sundays. Fridays may need to include a longer lunch break (sometimes finishing the morning session at 11.00 to 11.30 a.m.) to accommodate Muslim prayers. It's useful to talk to participants about the precise timings.

Ethiopian Orthodox Christians fast regularly on Wednesdays and Fridays. Some Christians also fast during Lent, Advent, and the Feast of the Flight from Egypt. Fasting may mean not consuming meat or dairy products. Muslims fast for the period of Ramadan during daylight. If possible, training should be avoided over fasting periods as participants are likely to be tired.

Key dates to avoid include:

> 7 January – Ethiopian Christmas or *Genna*
> 19 January – Epiphany or *Timket*
> 2 March – Victory of Adwa
> 1 May – International Labour Day
> 5 May – Ethiopian Patriots' Victory Day or *Arbegnoch Qen*
> 28 May – Downfall of the Derg (or Dergue)
> 11/12 September – Ethiopian New Year or *Enkutatash*
> 27 September – The Finding of the True Cross or *Meskel*

Dates vary:

> Orthodox Good Friday and Easter Day – around March/April, usually later than the non-Orthodox Easter
> Ramadan, Eid al-Fitr (End of Ramadan) and Eid al-Adha (Feast of Sacrifice)
> Birthday of the Prophet Mohammed (PBUH) or *Moulid*

Culture and time

Ethiopia follows its own calendar. This is seven to eight years behind the Western calendar. The government use this calendar so check your understanding when fixing dates. Time can also be different where Ethiopia uses the 12-hour clock, starting at 6.00 a.m. So, starting at 9.00 a.m., can be referred to as starting at 3.00 p.m. People refer to 'Ethiopian' or 'European' time, so always check.

Building rapport

It is important to establish a personal relationship with participants. Therefore, try to greet each person as they arrive, and find out their name and which organization they are from. Participants will want to know who you are and that they can understand you easily. Speak slower and more clearly than you would normally, to allow participants to 'tune in' to your voice and accent.

Conversation topics

Try to avoid religion and politics, and do not express strong opinions before you know the views of the other person. Ethiopians may not feel able to express their views in public. Avoid asking about ethnic backgrounds, and anything about sexual matters. Football is a good topic of conversation, especially for men – Ethiopians follow a number of the United Kingdom Premier League football clubs. Ask about a person's culture, community, their family, work, and topics they are interested in.

Ethiopians are aware of an outside perception of their country as one needing development and emergency aid. Avoid mentioning this and be sensitive if this is raised in conversation by others.

Training tips

- Ethiopians often speak softly and you should follow their lead.
- Situations are sometimes exaggerated to make a point, and you can do so too if telling an anecdote or story. Be careful not to go too far and lose your credibility.
- Be practical rather than theoretical. Make sure the learning is applied to the participants' situations. Try to avoid using examples from elsewhere in the world, instead adapt them to the Ethiopian context.
- Do not make anyone lose face. Do not confront or criticize people, especially in front of others.
- Ask challenging questions that will make participants really think. Give them time to answer.
- Use lots of group work.
- It is usual to have a fun introductory activity to help participants to get to know each other, and you.
- Ethiopians love to laugh, so have fun.

Training in Ghana

If someone does not know, someone teaches (Akan proverb).

There are many ethnic groups in Ghana. The largest are: Akan, Moshi-Dagbani, Ewe, and Ga. The words used in this section are from the largest Akan (Twi) language. Check which languages participants speak as their first language, and find a few more words to use as well.

Greetings

Greetings are considered important in Ghana and should not be rushed. You will be expected to acknowledge and greet people as you meet them at the start of a training course and at other gatherings. Older people are granted greater respect and should be greeted first. Generally, look people in the eye and greet them with a handshake and a smile. Greeting with handshakes is more common with men. Ghanaian women are less likely to offer their hand when greeting, but may respond to one offered. If greeting several people with a handshake, go from right to left.

Failing to greet people can be considered an insult. Ask about the health of the person you meet and also about the health of

Box 7.4 Fact file: Ghana

Full name	Republic of Ghana
Capital	Accra
National population	31,072,940 (Accra: 1,963,264)
Land area	227,540 square kilometres
Main language(s) Dagme Muslims),	English (national language), Akan (Twi), Daggare, (Adangme), Ga, Ewe, Gonja, Hausa (particularly for Kasem and Nzema). Also, Pidgin English is spoken
Predominant religion	Christian (69%), Muslim (16%) – mostly in the north
Currency	Ghana cedi (GHS or GH¢). The cedi is divided into 100 Ghanaian pesewa (Gp). The cedi was redenominated in 2007 and divided by 10,000. Some Ghanaians still quote the old amount
Time	GMT
Telephone code	+ 233

their family members. Sometimes your hand will be held loosely while the greetings take place. Some Ghanaians, especially men, will also snap the fingers at the end of a handshake, as a sign of friendship. This is usually not practised in a strictly professional setting, but can occur in informal settings or as you become more familiar with your participants. Learning how to snap back can build familiarity. In rural areas, it is polite to say 'hello' to people you pass, but this tends not to happen in the cities.

Words of greeting

Start every encounter with a spoken greeting, for example *Eti sen* (hello) or *Maa-chi* (good morning). People like to be greeted by name.

Business cards

Business cards are given out freely. Give cards with the right hand or with both hands together. Do not use the left hand.

Course certificates

Ghanaian participants will want to receive a certificate at the end of a training that confirms their participation. Present certificates with your right hand or with both hands together.

Names

Call Ghanaians by their professional or academic title (if they have one) and their family name. Younger people may ask you to call them by their first name soon after meeting. Older people wait until you have established a good relationship before moving to first names.

A full Ghanaian name will include a first name and a family name, but most Ghanaians will also have at least one middle name. A very common form of middle name is one that corresponds to the day of the week a person is born. Most Ghanaian ethnic groups have male and female names for each day of the week. For example, Kofi and Afia are male and female names respectively for a person born on a Friday among parts of the Akan ethnic group.

Gender and equality

Men tend to be more dominant in Ghanaian society. However, many women are independent and have important roles in the workplace. Trainers should make sure that equal opportunities for participation are offered to both men and women in training sessions.

Language

Some words in Akan (Twi):

Hello/how are you? – *Eti sen*
Welcome – *Akwaaba*
How are you? – *Wo ho te sen?* And the response – *Me ho ye* (I am fine)
Thank you (very much) – *Me da see (paa)*
Goodbye – *Nante yie*
Good/fine – *Eye* (pronounced *eyer*)
Well done – *Ayikoo*

Dress for the trainer

Smart casual dress is required for trainers. Suits may be needed for men and women attending government or formal events. On Fridays, some organizations encourage their staff to wear traditionally Ghanaian attire. This could be a simple attire (such as a shirt, dress, blouse) made from Ghanaian print fabric. While this is certainly not required, it will be appreciated if the host organization has such a requirement. Check with your local contact.

Working week and holidays

Working hours are generally from 8.00 a.m. to 5.00 p.m. with a break for lunch. Training days would normally start at 9.00 a.m. and end at 5.00 p.m. with breaks in the morning, at lunchtime, and in the afternoon.

Key dates to avoid include:

1 January – New Year
6 March – Independence Day

1 May – May Day/International Labour Day
25 May – Africa Union Day
1 July – Republic Day
21 September – Founder's Day (Kwame Nkrumah's birthday)
First Friday in December – Farmers' Day
25 and 26 December – Christmas holiday

Dates vary:

Good Friday and Easter Monday – usually during March or April
Ramadan, Eid-al-Fitr and Eid al-Adha – linked to the Muslim calendar

Culture and time

Family ties are very important in Ghana. Loyalty is primarily to family members. Respect is given to people with seniority in organizations or older people more generally. The culture of punctuality varies across organizations in Ghana. Trainers should stress that sessions will start on time and follow the agreed timetable. But allow some extra time in sessions to accommodate possible delays.

Building rapport

Try to talk with each of the participants and find out more about them, in order to build rapport. Show interest in their wellbeing and share your own work and personal experiences.

Conversation topics

Ghanaians are typically friendly people, especially when you have got to know them a little. Talk with them about where they are from and what they do, as well as their family. Be careful, however, not to make comments about a particular ethnic group. Many men are keen on football. Religion and politics can be talked about, but do not express strong views before you know what the other person thinks.

Training tips

- Saving face and not losing face are important in Ghana. It is therefore crucial not to do anything that would embarrass a course participant. Generally, people would rather remain silent to avoid embarrassing themselves or someone else.
- When training within one organization, accept that the most senior person often speaks on behalf of the whole group. Try breaking into smaller groups to collect all participants' views when they report back.
- Ghanaians like to have fun. Encourage them to tell stories if they want to, and try to organize some enjoyable activities as part of the training.
- Do not be concerned if Ghanaians tease you. Enjoy it and take it as a compliment as it means the person is relaxed in your company.

Training in India

Live as if you were to die tomorrow, learn as if you were to live forever (Mahatma Gandhi).

India has many different regions, languages, religious beliefs, and cultures. It is more like a continent in scale, than a country. This section gives general information, but look out for differences between, and within, states in language and culture. If in doubt, check with your Indian contact.

Greetings

It is common to shake hands, especially in the big cities. It may not be appropriate to do this with the opposite sex. If you are a man, wait for a woman to offer a hand. There is little contact between men and women in public, so hugs and kisses on the cheek, for example, are not appropriate. However, men sometimes hold hands with men, and women with women. Westernized Indians are likely to break some of these rules. A traditional greeting throughout India is the *Namaste*. Put your hands together just below your chin and close to your body, and nod your head slightly. This is sometimes followed by a handshake.

Box 7.5 Fact file: India

Full name	Republic of India
Capital	New Delhi
National population	1,380,004,385 (Delhi: 10,927,986)
Land area	2,973,190 square kilometres
Main language(s)	Hindi (national language), English (associate official language). Other languages include: Assamese, Bengali, Gujarati, Kannada, Kashmiri, Malayalam, Marathi, Oriya, Punjabi, Sanskrit, Sindhi, Tamil, Telugu, and Urdu
Predominant religions	Hindu 81%, Muslim 12%, Sikh 2%, Christian 2%
Currency	Indian rupee (₹, Rs or INR) divided into 100 paisa
Time	GMT + 5.5 hours
Telephone code	+ 91

Words of greeting

The most common greeting is *Namaste* or *Namaskar* (or their equivalent in other parts of India), together with the *Namaste* greeting. The response is the same. If working with Muslim participants, the greeting is usually *Assalaam alaikum* and the response *Valaikum salaam*. For Sikh participants, it is *Sat sri akal*, and the response is the same. India has many different languages – 22 officially recognized. Find out, in advance, the predominant language of your participants, and check the appropriate greeting for them.

Business cards

Business cards are very important in India. If you have an Indian cell/mobile phone number, write it on the back of the card. Course participants will expect you to have enough cards to give them one each. Offer them and receive them with your right hand, and make sure it's the right way around, so the person receiving your card can read it. It would be usual to make a comment on a piece of information on receiving a card, for example 'where did you study for your BA?'

Course certificates

Present certificates with your right hand.

Names

Indian names and their order differ depending on cultural background and religion. In north India, the given name is usually followed by the family name. For example, Rajesh Sharma, with Rajesh the given name. In other parts, the given name is likely to be at the end, with the father's name and possibly a place name preceding it. These names can be written as initials before the given name, for example K.V. Rama. Indians can sometimes be formal and for foreigners include 'Mr', 'Mrs', 'Miss', or 'Ms' before a given or family name whenever they speak to you. If you want to show respect to someone older or more senior, you should do the same. It is usual to include any rank or title when addressing someone, for example Dr Sharma. Always ask participants what they would like to be called at the beginning of the training.

Gender and equality

Groups of men and women from the cities are likely to be happy mixing with each other, but female participants from rural areas may not feel comfortable contributing to a large group discussion. In this situation, consider using a female trainer and/or someone who is sensitive to gender issues. Participants of the same sex often sit together at mealtime and in breaks. While you may want to mix groups up in the training sessions, this can mean participants do not fully concentrate. Accept where participants choose to sit for the first day or two of the training. If you want to move them, do so when they feel more settled.

Language

English is spoken widely, but it can take some time for course participants to understand your accent or what you are saying. This is particularly the case outside the main urban areas, and with those who understand English but do not use it regularly. It is likely that no one will want to embarrass you, or themselves, by mentioning that they do not understand what you are saying. Speak slightly slower and more clearly than you would do normally. Ask the group in the early stages of the course 'how are you finding my English?' Talk with them during the breaks to check that you are communicating in a way that they can understand. Some speakers of English as a second or third language often understand what is being said, but are not so confident to speak.

Some words in Hindi:

> Hello – *Namaste* or *Namaskar*
> Welcome – *Swagatham*
> How are you? – *Aap Kaise Hain?*
> Thank you (very much) – (*Bahut*) *Bahut Dhanyawad*
> Goodbye – *Phir milenge* (informal) or *Namaskar*
> Good/fine – *Accha*
> Well done – *Bahut Acche*

Dress for the trainer

For government or corporate training events, more formal wear is appropriate. A suit and tie are appropriate for men, and a smart dress (sometimes a sari) or trousers for women. For the non-profit sector, smart casual wear is appropriate. However, being too casual can be seen as not being professional, and your words may not be taken seriously. It is good for men and women to wear long sleeves, and for women to keep the majority of their legs covered. Dressing modestly is important whatever the weather, especially outside the main cities.

Working week and holidays

The working week is from Monday to Friday, often working between 9.00 a.m. and 6.00 p.m. Many organizations expect their staff to work additional hours. Participants attending a course in their home town may still go into their office after the course. Some may want to keep their phones on, in case of office emergencies, throughout the course. Courses generally run from 9.00 a.m. to 5.00 p.m., with an hour for lunch and refreshment breaks in the morning and afternoon.

Key dates to avoid include:

26 January – Republic Day
15 August – Independence Day
2 October – Gandhi's Birthday
22 November – Guru Nanak's Birthday, for the Sikh community
25 December – Christmas Day, for the Christian community.

Dates vary:

Diwali – for Hindus is in October/November. This is preceded 20 days before by the Dussehra festival
Ramadan – a month of fasting for Muslims, followed by Eid ul-Fitr
Good Friday and Easter Day – for Christians, usually March or April
State and regional festivals take place – check with your Indian contact

Culture and time

Indians expect their trainers to be punctual. However, participants are not always on time and can rearrange meetings at the last minute. Stress the course start times, and encourage participants to be on time. However, do not be too worried if one or two participants arrive late.

Building rapport

Personal relationships are very important in India. Talking with participants individually and as a group is a good way to build trust. A fun introductory activity at the beginning of the training will be appreciated. Do not feel bad if things do not work as you had planned; seeing the human side of someone helps to build trust. Make sure the course feels safe, so that participants know they will not lose face or feel embarrassed. Participants will want to know your qualification for training them. Someone may introduce you at the beginning of the course. If they do not, give a brief summary of your background and include a short biography of yourself and other trainers with the handouts.

Conversation topics

If you are a non-Indian, participants will often ask your name, country of origin, what you do, your marital status and how many children you have. Have answers ready for these. Sometimes you are asked how much you earn – plan a vague response for this last question! Conversation topics can include politics, family and children, travel, movies, and sport. Keep up to date with the latest cricket and football results, if you can. It is best to avoid personal issues, relationships, corruption, or to express strong opinions about politics or religion.

Training tips

- However good the advance planning, preparation for a course can still be last minute, but will get done. It is worth checking, however, that things will be prepared as you want them. This includes the layout of the room, equipment, and handouts. Otherwise, incorrect assumptions can be made.
- *Jugaad* is a useful technique. It refers to finding solutions for delivering what is needed, using minimum resources. It can also mean finding a person who can solve a difficult problem. This can help you to arrange whatever you want. *Jugaad* is recognized as being almost a management technique in India.
- Use local examples whenever possible. Be careful not to quote too many events from your own country or participants may think or say 'but that wouldn't work in India'.
- Sometimes people from India move their heads from side to side as a sign of respect, or simply to mean 'maybe' or 'I understand'.
- Trainers have a high status in India, especially international trainers. If you are coming from a culture where ideas are constantly questioned, you must be careful to make sure that what you are saying is acceptable in an Indian context.
- Indians can challenge the trainer. Be polite and courteous when challenged, and recognize the truth in what is said, even if you disagree or want to put forward another viewpoint.
- Remember always to save face.

- There are many vegetarians in India, especially in South India. Food for training events should be prepared and labelled clearly for both vegetarian and non-vegetarian participants.
- Allow plenty of time for questions and discussion.

Training in Jordan

It is always dangerous to underestimate anybody (King Abdullah II)

Greetings

Jordanians will greet each other formally when they meet. The same sex will shake hands, with everyone in the group, and sometimes kiss on the cheeks. Usually, Jordanians will not physically greet members of the opposite sex, so wait for the other person to offer their hand to you. If a woman or a man puts a hand on their chest, it is also a sign of respect or greeting, but means they do not want to shake hands with someone of the opposite sex for religious reasons. Sometimes people will touch your arm or shoulder as a sign of affection.

Box 7.6 Fact file: Jordan

Full name	The Hashemite Kingdom of Jordan
Capital	Amman
National population	10,203,134 (Amman: 1,275,857)
Land area	88,780 square kilometres
Main language(s)	Arabic (official) and English
Predominant religions	Muslim 92%, Christian 6%
Currency	Jordanian dinar (JOD or JD) divided into 100 qirsh (or piastres)
Time	GMT + 2 hours (October to March)
	GMT + 3 hours (April to September)
Telephone code	+ 962

Words of greeting

The traditional greeting is *Al salamu alaykum* (peace be upon you), and the reply is *Wa aleikum as-salam* (and upon you be peace). The more informal *Marhaba* means 'hi'. *Salaam* is also used as a greeting. You could also use *Sabah al-Khayr* (good morning) or *Masa al-Khayr* (good afternoon).

Business cards

Have plenty of business cards to give out when you meet people and to give to course participants. Offer cards with your right hand.

Course certificates

Present certificates with your right hand.

Names

Use titles of people when you use their names (for example Mr, Ms, Doctor) to show respect, especially in the government sector. Younger people would generally call each other by their first name. Ask course participants what they would like to be called at the start of the course.

Gender and equality

Women have achieved more equality in Jordan than in other countries in the Middle East. Therefore, it is likely that both sexes will fully participate in a training event. However, avoid activities and energizers that require participants to touch, or be in close proximity to, each other.

Language

A frequent Arabic expression that is used is *in sha' Allah* (God willing). Islam encourages people to see everything that happens as due to God's will. This is used as an answer to a number of questions and frustrations. In Jordan, people will be delighted if you try a few words of Arabic, even if your pronunciation is not perfect.

Some words in Arabic:

Hello – *Marhaba* (informal)
Welcome – *Ahlan wa sahlan* with a reply *Ahlan Feek* (also used to mean hello)
How are you? – *Keefak* (to a male) or *Keefek* (to a female) and the reply *Al-Hamdu lillah* (fine, literally 'thanks be to God')
Thank you (very much) – *Shukran* (*Kteer*)
Goodbye – *Ma'a salama*
Good/fine – *Jayyed* (male) or *Jayyeda* (female)
Well done – *Ahsant* (male), *Ahsanti* (female), or *Mumtaz* ('excellent')

Dress for the trainer

Be respectful and modest in your dress. Generally, men and women should wear long sleeved shirts or blouses, with trousers or a long skirt, for women. Amman tends to be more liberal in dress, but consider where people attending the course are coming from. Shorts or short skirts are not acceptable for trainers, and could undermine your credibility.

Working week and holidays

Government office hours are usually from 8.00 a.m. to 3.00 p.m. The working week is from Sunday to Thursday, with many offices having Friday and Saturday as the weekend. Some of the working hours are shorter during the fasting month of Ramadan. Training days would normally be from 9.00 a.m. to 5.00 p.m., with breaks in the morning, afternoon, and for lunch.

Key dates to avoid include:

1 January – New Year's Day
1 May – Labour Day
25 May – Jordan's Independence Day
25 December – Christmas Day (only for Christians)

Dates vary:

Ramadan – month of fasting
Eid al-Fitr, Eid al-Adha, Al-Mawled Al-Nabawi (Prophet Muhammad's Birthday (PBUH)) and Islamic New Year – dates according to the lunar calendar
Easter – usually March or April (only for Christians)

Culture and time

In Jordanian culture time and deadlines are flexible. Be on time yourself at the start of every training session, but be aware that others might not be. Be aware of this when planning the training.

Jordanians use a lot of hand movements when talking. Sometimes instead of saying 'no' to something, they can move their eyebrows and head upwards and make a 'tsk' sound.

Putting your right hand over your heart means 'no thanks'. People may give you limited eye contact, especially females. This is often a sign of respect.

Building rapport

Do not forget to greet people as they arrive each day. This builds rapport with the trainer. People who have been educated in Europe and North America are treated as more knowledgeable than people educated in the Middle East. Age and experience are respected as well. Honesty and giving sincere compliments are important and will also help build rapport.

Conversation topics

Ask about the country and the Jordanian culture and history. Express what you appreciate about their country. Also ask about participants' families and any children they have. Other topics include food, music, and places in Jordan. Be careful not to express strong views about politics, religion, gender, or the royal family. Jordanians can ask you about your own faith. Avoid any type of criticism even if only implied.

Training tips

- Find out about the Jordanian culture. Give examples in your training that relate to Jordan or the countries that the participants are from. Avoid using examples from your home country.
- When using humour, make sure it does not criticize another person.
- If participants are speaking to each other in Arabic, a non-speaker may feel that it sounds more heated than it

actually is. If there is conflict, it is usually brought to a conclusion quickly.
- Jordanians like to be polite with one another and will not criticize someone directly, no matter how small. If you need to talk with someone about a behavioural issue, always do it privately. The same applies when giving negative feedback.
- Jordan, and Amman in particular, is often used as a centre for training events for other countries in the Middle East. Find out where your participants are from, and try to find out about their culture, too.

Training in Kenya

He who is unable to dance says that the yard is stony (Masai proverb).

Greetings

Shaking hands is common, with a firm handshake often followed by a 'Kenyan handshake'. This involves clasping the thumbs and then returning to a handshake. This can be done several times. The handshake can take a few minutes especially if you already know the person. Sometimes, the left hand is placed on top of your own and the other person's hand. This shows

Box 7.7 Fact file: Kenya

Full names	The Republic of Kenya
Capital	Nairobi
National population	53,771,296 (Nairobi: 2,750,547)
Land area	569,140 square kilometres
Main language(s)	Kiswahili (national and official), English (official). Other languages include: Dholuo (or Luo), Kikuyu, and Luhya
Predominant religion	Christian (78%), Muslim (10%)
Currency	Kenya shilling (KSh or KES) divided into 100 cents
Time	GMT + 3 hours
Telephone code	+ 254

warmth and affection. To show additional respect, place you left hand on your right elbow as you shake hands. This gesture can also be used if you give or receive something. Muslims do not always shake hands with the opposite sex. A man should wait to be offered a hand when greeting a female Muslim. It is usual to ask the other person 'how are you?' If you know the person reasonably well, you might also ask about their family. Greetings should not be rushed, especially outside the cities.

In Kenya, hands are shaken often, so join in and enjoy it. If you or someone else says something amusing, you will usually be offered a hand to shake to share the joke more fully. Sometimes a 'high five' can replace the handshake. If someone has dirty or wet hands, no problem, they will offer a wrist or forearm to shake instead.

Words of greeting

Usually *jambo* ('hello') just before you shake hands. This can be followed by *habari* ('hello, how are you'), with the reply *nzuri* ('fine'). English words of greeting are also used.

Business cards

Business cards are usually presented as part of an initial meeting. Course participants are likely to ask you for one. Present or receive the card with the right hand, or both hands together, but not with the left hand alone.

Course certificates

Present certificates with your right hand, or both hands together, but not with just the left hand.

Names

First names are often taken from the family's religion. Second names are given by the parents, and finally a family name (usually the father's). It is not unusual for Kenyans to call someone by their second or family name. So always ask participants what they would like to be called. For those you do not know well, or want to show more respect to, it is acceptable to use their title followed by their first name (for example Mrs Ruth, Dr Mohammed).

Gender and equality

In rural areas, more effort may be needed to make sure that women participate fully in the training. This can be easier for a female trainer to achieve. This is less likely to be an issue in urban areas with younger and more educated participants. Always make sure you encourage both women and men to report back on group work.

Language

Most people speak at least some English. It is widely spoken in urban areas, but less so in rural areas.
Some words in Kiswahili:

Hello – *Jambo*
Welcome – *Karibu* ('you are welcome')
How are you? – *Habari yako* or just *Habari*, the reply is *Nzuri*
Thank you (very much) – *Asante (Sana)*
Goodbye – *Kwaheri*
Good/fine – *Nzuri*
Well done – *Hongera*

Dress for the trainer

Dress modestly. Tight clothing or jeans are not appropriate, especially in rural areas. Make sure your shoulders and knees are covered. If training for government workers and sometimes commercial organizations, a more formal dress is appropriate. For example, a suit and tie for men, and full length dress or long trousers with a smart top for women. For non-profit organizations, smart casual dress is more usual. Avoid shorts.

Working week and holidays

Working hours are between 8.30 a.m. and 5.00 p.m. Training courses would usually start at 9.00 a.m. and finish at around

4.30 p.m. Lunch breaks are for an hour, sometimes longer. Refreshment breaks are usually around 10.00 a.m. and 3.00 p.m. Although sometimes people arrive late for meetings, they are mostly on time for courses. Throughout the training, it is worth emphasizing when you want people to arrive, and to return from breaks. It is useful to plan the course material so it would still work if a few of the participants are not there at the start of each session.

The working week for Kenyans runs from Monday to Friday, but can also include Saturday morning. You can find that participants who live locally go back to their office after the training. Sunday is a rest day and many people will attend worship. Christian and Muslim holidays are acknowledged, as well as Hindu and Sikh festivals.

Key dates to avoid include:

1 January – New Year's Day
1 May – Labour Day
1 June – Madaraka (Self-rule) Day
20 October – Mashujaa (or Hero's Day)
12 December – Jamhuri (Independence) Day
25 and 26 December – Christmas Day and Boxing Day

Dates vary:

Good Friday, and Easter Day, followed by the Easter Monday holiday – usually March or April
Ramadan, the month of fasting followed by the Id-ul-Fitr feast, the first day of this is an official holiday for Muslims

Culture and time

Nairobi is a regional centre as well as the capital. International approaches to business are common, for example being punctual for meetings. However, the heavy traffic in the capital sometimes makes punctuality difficult to achieve. Outside Nairobi there is often a higher temperature and life is at a slower pace.

Faith is important to Kenyans. Churches and mosques are full and often run many worship services in the cities. Often training events and meetings will start and end with prayer. Occasionally a trainer is expected to lead this.

A Kenyan tradition is that people should all have their say, which goes back to life in local communities. It is always a challenge to allow participants to say what they want but to avoid taking too long.

Building rapport

Establish good relationships between the trainer(s) and the group. Share stories with the group and be open to allowing the participants to share their own stories as part of the course. Try to use Kenyan stories when possible, or otherwise do not be too specific about where the events took place. Use a fun activity to help the group introduce themselves to each other and to the trainers.

Conversation topics

Few topics are considered taboo for Kenyans. A popular topic is the weather and if it has or will rain. Kenyans sometimes say 'it is promising rain' and treat rain as a blessing from God, as it's such an important part of their life. Other topics include sport, especially football, culture, family, food, work, and national politics, if you know the person reasonably well.

However, do not express strong opinions about politics. Be especially careful around election times. Avoid tribal politics altogether, as well as sexual matters. Try not to be too direct and always aim to save face – both the other person's and your own.

Training tips

- It is useful if you are new to Kenya to ask someone, who the group may know and respect, to introduce you to them at the beginning of the event.
- Kenyans like to work in groups. There is a strong culture of mutual responsibility and self-reliance. Encourage groups to work together, and to be responsible for the work they produce.
- When introducing new ways of working to an organization, give a brief summary of how they have been working so far, before explaining why a change is necessary. Also, allow participants to ask questions before agreeing how the new practices can be introduced.

- If possible, celebrate the success of completing the training event together with the participants.

Training in Pakistan

Learn from your cradle to your grave (Prophet Muhammad (PBUH)).

Greetings

Men tend to shake hands on meeting and also at the beginning of each day. Women almost never shake hands. Wait for others to offer their hand. Putting your right hand over your heart is also a greeting in some areas of Pakistan and is sometimes used as a greeting if you are not close enough to shake hands.

Hugging is used between two males and between two females, but only when a good working relationship has been formed. If someone hugs you at the end of a course, you will know you have made a favourable impression.

Words of greeting

A common greeting is: *Assalamu alaikum* ('peace be upon you'). The reply is: *Waalaikum assalam* ('and upon you be peace').

Box 7.8 Fact file: Pakistan

Full name	Islamic Republic of Pakistan
Capital	Islamabad
National population	220,892,340 (Islamabad: 601,600)
Land area	770,880 square kilometres
Main language(s)	English (official) and Urdu (national). Others include: Baluchi, Baruhi, Hindku, Kashmiri, Punjabi, Pushto, Saraiki, and Sindhi
Predominant religion	Muslim (97%)
Currency	Pakistani rupees (Rs or PKR) divided into 100 paisa.
Time	GMT + 5 hours
Telephone code	+ 92

This is said upon meeting each day. An alternative is *Soobh bakhair*, meaning good morning. Sometimes people will also greet international visitors in English.

Business cards

Cards are regularly presented upon meeting for the first time. You are likely to be asked for your card in training courses too. If you leave a pile of these somewhere discreetly, you will find most of them are taken by the end of the course. Give and receive cards with your right hand only. When you receive someone's card, it is polite to read it for a few moments and perhaps ask a question, before putting it away safely and respectfully. Avoid putting it away casually, as this would be seen as discourteous.

Course certificates

Present certificates with your right hand.

Names

Three names are usually used in Pakistan, with the family name either first or last. At the beginning of the training, ask participants to write the name they want to be called on a 'name card'. Stress that you only want their 'known by' name, so it is easier for you to learn.

If you want to show respect, particularly on the first day of the training, use 'Mr', 'Ms', or 'Mrs' before the name, especially for more senior and older participants. The Pakistani version of showing respect to older men is *Sahib*, meaning sir, and to senior women either ma'am or more formally *Begam sahiba*, meaning madam. These can be used before the family name.

Gender and equality

It is important to be sensitive about gender issues. Make sure any training activities are equally accessible for both men and women. Avoid icebreakers or energizers that require physical contact between men and women, especially outside urban areas. Use group work to encourage everyone to be able to participate equally. Encourage women to present during feedback sessions. In rural areas, a female trainer may be more appropriate, especially one who speaks the local language. However, in rural areas, some male participants may not accept a female trainer, so take this into account before deciding who will run the course. Talk with your local contact.

Language

English is the language of government and business, and is widely spoken in urban areas. It is spoken by most professional people, although in training events the level of English can vary. In urban areas, it is not usually necessary to have an interpreter, but the trainer must speak clearly and slowly. In rural areas, an interpreter may be needed, if it is not possible to have a trainer who speaks the language.

Some words in Urdu:

Hello – *Assalamu alaikum*
Welcome – *Khush āmdīd*
How are you? – *Aap khairiyat se hain?*
Thank you (very much) – *Shukriya* (or *Mehrbani*)
Goodbye – *Khuda hafiz* or *Allah hafiz*
Good/fine – *Bohat umda*
Well done – *Shabaash*

Dress for the trainer

Dress modestly. Men tend to dress in dark colours. Men should wear smart casual clothes when training or attending meetings within the non-profit sector. For government and business, men wear ties and usually suits. Women should wear long-sleeved, loose-fitting tops and a long, loose skirt. A head scarf is not mandatory in urban areas, but a scarf can be loosely hung around the neck or over the chest. However, always wear a head scarf in rural areas. If female trainers wear traditional dress, the *shalwar kameez*, they are likely to develop a better rapport more quickly with participants, male and female. Women should avoid heavy makeup, perfume, or a lot of jewellery.

Working week and holidays

Although Friday is the holy day in Pakistan, the working week runs from Monday to Friday, and possibly half of Saturday. Some organizations will work for only half a day on Friday, but most will allow an extended lunch break (perhaps an extra 30 minutes) to allow time for prayers. Sunday will nearly always be a rest day.

Timing for training will often be from 9.00 a.m. to 5.00 p.m. with breaks, although some courses will start earlier. If training on a Friday, it is important to talk sensitively with the organization or group about the best timing to allow participants to attend prayers.

There are three types of public holiday: those observed nation-wide; those observed only in particular provinces; and those observed by a particular faith community.

Key dates to avoid include:

> 5 February – Kashmir Day
> 23 March - Pakistan Day – passing of the Pakistan resolution in 1940
> 1 May – Labour Day
> 14 August – Independence Day
> 25 December – Birthday of Jinnah

Dates vary:

> Ramadan varies each year according to the Muslim calendar. It is followed by Eid ul-Fitr (also known as the 'small Eid'), which is a three-day public holiday.

There are several other important religious holidays, observed according to the Muslim calendar. The most important ones are:

> *Eid ul-Azha* or 'Feast of Sacrifice', eight days into the Hajj pilgrimage month lasting for 3 days or more
> *Ashura*, eight days into the first month of the Muslim Hijra calendar, Muharram lasting for 2 days.
> *Eid-e-Milad-un-Nabi*, birthday of Prophet Muhammad (PBUH), on the 12th day of the third month of the Hijra calendar. It lasts one day.

Culture and time

Good timekeeping is seen as a professional standard. But participants occasionally arrive late. The trainer should be tolerant of latecomers, and explain what they missed during the break. At the end of each day, state the time you intend to begin the following day, and stress that participants should arrive promptly.

Building rapport

People in Pakistan like to have training, and it is considered to be a high-status occasion, especially with an international trainer. Try to have someone to introduce the trainer at the beginning and refer to their role, experience, and background. If no one is available to do this, the trainer should explain this themselves. A business card showing your qualifications helps to reinforce this.

Conversation topics

Try to avoid expressing strong views, especially about religion and politics, and be open to what others have to say. Suitable topics are food, culture, sport, especially cricket, and Bollywood and Hollywood films. Ask about the family in general but do not ask directly about specific family members.

Training tips

- Keep your language clear and simple. Although many participants have excellent English, they can struggle with complex or technical words in English. Ask participants to tell you if they do not understand.
- Participants respond well to interactive activities and training games.
- Use examples from Pakistan in the training, rather than examples from another country. It helps participants feel the training is relevant to them.
- Observe a voluntary silence, as a mark of respect, when the *Aadhaan* – the call to prayer – is made on a loudspeaker from a nearby mosque. It can happen twice during each training day, in the early and late afternoon.
- Watch for the sideways tilt of the head, which is often a way of saying 'yes'.

- Sometime Pakistanis say 'no' by making a 'tsk' sound, sometimes with raised eyebrows, and a flick of the head backwards.
- Often a senior person is expected to open (and close) the workshop. Check whether this will happen and, if so, allow time for some speeches on the first day.
- Courses in Pakistan are usually great fun, so enjoy the experience.

Training in United Kingdom

> *It's all to do with training: you can do a lot if you're properly trained (Queen Elizabeth II).*

The United Kingdom is made up of four countries: England, Northern Ireland, Scotland, and Wales. 'Great Britain' refers to the countries on the main island: England, Scotland, and Wales, together with a number of small islands. Northern Ireland is situated on the neighbouring island of Ireland. There are regional cultural differences between the countries of the United Kingdom, and differences too between the people from a variety of ethnic backgrounds. London and other large cities are very multicultural and multi-racial.

Greetings

Usually a hand shake and a smile. British people do not always bother with a handshake, but will respond if a hand is offered. A hug, or a kiss, on one or sometimes both cheeks, is exchanged between friends and family, and sometimes for work colleagues. This is mainly between women, or between a man and a woman. Occasionally men will hug each other, but it is more common for them just to shake hands. Use some eye contact with people you meet, but do not overuse it.

Words of greeting

Hello, or Hi, and good morning (or just 'morning'). Good afternoon or good evening at the appropriate times of day are more formal and less frequently used. How do you do? (or sometimes How are you?) is a formal phrase sometimes used

Box 7.9 Fact file: United Kingdom

Full name	United Kingdom of Great Britain and Northern Ireland (UK for short)
Capital	London
National population	67,886,011 (London: 7,556,900)
Land area	241,930 square kilometres
Main language(s)	English (official), Gaelic (Gàidhlig or Ghaeilge) in parts of Scotland and Northern Ireland, Welsh (Cymraeg) in parts of Wales. Most Gaelic and Welsh speakers also speak English
Predominant religion	Christian – Protestant and Catholic, and significant numbers of other faiths – Hindu, Jewish, Muslim and Sikh
Currency–	Pound sterling (£) split into 100 pence (p)
Time	GMT (late March to late October GMT + 1)
Telephone code	+ 44

when shaking hands. It doesn't need a reply, but possibly a slight nod of acknowledgement.

Business cards

Business cards are often exchanged between professionals. It is a compliment if someone asks you for one. Generally, people will not examine the card, but just put it to one side. Do not feel insulted by this.

Course certificates

Present a certificate with one or two hands. Certificates are often given with the left hand, while shaking the person's hand with the right hand.

Names

Usually the given name followed by the family name. People from other cultures living in the UK often choose to follow this pattern, and sometimes will choose a new first name for themselves. It is usual that people will call each other by their first name, but older and more senior people sometimes prefer be called by their title (for example Mr, Ms or Dr) followed by their family name. At training events, ask participants what they want to be called.

Gender and equality

The United Kingdom has a tradition of equal rights between men and women. It is normal for men and women to mix freely at training events. However, be sensitive to participants from other traditions living in the UK. Workers in most organizations will show a sense of equality when attending a training event together. Most will speak freely.

Language

British people are often self-deprecating, and tease each other. Sometimes this is used to convey humour, although for someone not from this culture it can be confusing. Often achievements are understated and people are modest. Be careful if travelling outside England, that you do not use phrases like 'a full English breakfast'. Irish, Scottish or Welsh people can reply, 'I'm sorry we do not have that!' If you are training with bilingual participants in Northern Ireland, Scotland, or Wales, using a greeting in their language will endear you to them.

Some alternative words in English:

> Hello – or the more informal *Hi* or *Morning*
> Welcome – or *Thank you for being here today*
> How are you? – or *How's things?* The response is usually *Fine*, or *Good* from younger people.
> Thank you (very much) – or *Thanks a lot* and sometimes *Thanks so much*
> Goodbye – or *Cheerio, Bye,* or *See you soon*
> Good/fine – or *That's great*
> Well done – or *I really like that*

Other greetings:

> Scottish Gaelic: *Halò* (Hello), *Fàilte* (Welcome), *Ciamar a tha thu?* (singular) or *Ciamar a tha sibh?* (plural/polite)

(How are you?), response to 'how are you?' is *Tha gu math*, *Tapadh leat* (singular) or *Tapadh leibh* (plural) (Thank you (very much)), *Mar sin leat* (singular) or *Mar sin leibh* (plural) (Goodbye), *Glè mhath* (Good/fine), *Smath a rinn thu* (singular) or *Smath a rinn sibh* (plural) (Well done).

Welsh: *Helo* (hello), *Croeso* (Welcome), *Sut wyt ti?* (How are you?), the reply is *Iawn diolch*, *Diolch* (*yn fawr*) (Thank you (very much)), *Hwyl fawr* (Goodbye), *Da* (Good/fine), *Da iawn* (Well done).

Dress for the trainer

For most training events, smart casual wear is usual. If training in government or with senior managers, consider wearing more formal clothes, for example a suit or jacket. Do not wear shorts.

Working week and holidays

The working week is from Monday to Friday, traditionally from 9.00 a.m. to 5.00 p.m., although often employees are able to vary their working times, starting and finishing earlier or later.

Key dates to avoid include:

1 January – New Year's Day (and 2 January *in Scotland only*)
17 March (if falls at a weekend, the following Monday) – St Patrick's Day *in Northern Ireland only*
1 May – May Day (the first Monday in May is a holiday)
30 November (if falls at a weekend, the following Monday) – St Andrew's Day *in Scotland only*
25 December – Christmas Day
26 December – Boxing Day (the week after Christmas, up to and including New Year's Day, is a holiday for many)

Dates vary:

The dates of Good Friday, Easter Sunday, and Easter Monday are in March or April
The last Monday in May is Spring Bank Holiday

The first Monday in August is the summer bank holiday in Scotland. The last Monday in August is the summer bank holiday in the rest of the U.K.

People often take the whole of these weeks as holiday. People in the United Kingdom often refer to these dates as 'bank holidays'. The banks close on these days.

Culture and time

Be careful not to assume that everyone is English, although they do make up the majority. It is good to ask 'which part of the UK are you from?' Many people are also from a range of ethnic backgrounds and have settled in the UK over many years. The British, and especially the English, are always polite to each other. You will hear 'please', 'thank you', and 'sorry' many times over, often thanking someone for a minor favour, such as holding the door open for you. The British appreciate visitors saying 'please' and 'thank you' at appropriate times. People who work together cannot often socialize with each other, as they do not live close together. This is especially true in large cities. However, they may socialize by going for a drink (alcohol or coffee) after work, and by having a meal together in December to celebrate Christmas. When this happens people generally treat each other as equals rather than using any workplace hierarchy.

Participants are expected to be on time for meetings and training events, but not too early. The trainer would usually be expected to be there and set up the room at least half an hour before the event starts.

Building rapport

Trainers must be polite and tolerant and make sure that participants do not lose face. If someone is 'put down' when they ask a question of the trainer, everyone will notice this. This can lead to negative feelings about the trainer, although probably nothing will be said. Trainers should be knowledgeable about their subject but, outside academic circles, the British do not mind too much how this knowledge has been gained.

Conversation topics

British people often talk about the weather – not surprising as it is so changeable. Most topics of conversation are acceptable, but do not express strong opinions on politics or religion, until you know the other person's views. Many people in the U.K. do not practice a religious faith. Certainly, ask about a person's work, family and children, but do not assume anything. People can be married or live together with a partner of the opposite sex, or in a same-sex relationship. Football, cricket, and tennis are followed fanatically by some, and most people would have something to say about a major sporting event. British people can become embarrassed by personal questions, for example 'how much do you earn?' or their status within an organization, so avoid such questions until you know the person well.

Training tips

- Give plenty of notice of what you need for the training event. State clearly what you want. Usually everything will be prepared for you when you arrive, but it is worth checking if everything is ready a day or two beforehand.
- If an organization arranges the training event, it is usual for someone to introduce the trainer when it begins. However, this person may not stay for the whole day, but may come back to help you clear up. If they do, it is still good manners to help them do this at the end of the day. Sometimes the trainer is left to do everything by themselves.
- Most participants are usually happy to play a training game, as long as it is clear how it is relevant to the learning.
- Training administration is generally good. Check in advance that your host organization knows exactly what you require.
- People from the United Kingdom can be direct in their way of speaking. Do not be put off by this.
- Look out for British phrases that do not quite mean what they say, such as 'that's not bad' meaning it is good, or 'could I give you some feedback' meaning they want you to understand what they say and probably change your ways of doing things.

- The British like to have fun but their humour is not obvious so not always easy to understand.
- Remember to keep saying 'please' and 'thank you' when dealing with participants.

Training in Zambia

Consistency enables one to achieve their goals (Zambian proverb).

Greetings

Greetings are particularly important in Zambia. A handshake is usual at every meeting, followed by asking about the health of the person and their family. This ritual greeting is part of accepting you as a member of the group. It should not be rushed. The handshake can involve clapping together your cupped hands twice before shaking hands to show respect. It might also include a Zambian handshake, which includes shaking hands and then clasping the thumb and then back to a traditional handshake. Women shake hands with other women, but men and women often do not shake each other's hands. You can place your left hand on your right elbow as you

Box 7.10 Fact file: Zambia

Full name	Republic of Zambia
Capital	Lusaka
National population	18,383,955 (Lusaka: 1,267,440)
Land area	743,390 square kilometres
Main language(s)	English (official), Bemba, Kaonde, Lozi, Lunda, Luvale, Nyanja/Chewa and Tonga. English is widely spoken in urban areas
Predominant religion	Christian (95%)
Currency	Zambian kwacha (ZMK or ZK) divided into 100 ngwee (N)
Time	GMT + 2 hours
Telephone code	+ 260

shake hands to show more respect. Women will sometimes hug another woman but not usually in public. For Zambians, eye contact and looking someone directly in the eye is not common, especially if the person is older or from another culture.

Words of greeting

A friendly 'hello, how are you' in English is acceptable. It is good if you can find out a person's first language, and use some greeting words from that. For example, the following words can be used in Bemba: *Mulishani mukwai* or more simply *Shani* ('Hello'), *Mwashibukeni mukwai* ('Good morning'), *Mumwaikaleni mukwai* ('Good afternoon').

Business cards

Business cards are important in Zambia. They should be in English and exchanged when you meet someone. They can be left available for course participants to take, but generally it is better to give them to individuals yourself. Give them with the right hand or with both hands together.

Course certificates

Present certificates with your right hand or with both hands together.

Names

The order of names is usually the first name followed by the family name. However, with the Bema people, for example, their surname and first name may be very similar. Also, the order may sometimes be reversed – someone maybe named Chanda Mulenga, while another person is Mulenga Chanda. Some names may be the same for men and women. Most names have a meaning, but some participants may not want to explain what their names mean. Therefore, be careful if asking about this in an introductory activity. Always ask participants what they would like to be called.

Gender and equality

Do not expect physical contact between different genders when planning activities. In most situations, women will speak freely but make sure that everyone is able to contribute if this is not the case.

Language

Some words in Bemba:

Hello – *Shani* or *Mulishani mukwai* (to show more respect)
Welcome – *Mwaiseni*
How are you? – *Mulishani mukwai*? The reply is *Bwino nga imwe mulishani*
Thank you (very much) – *Natotela sana mkayi*
Goodbye – *Shalapo* (informal – to a younger person) or *Shalenipo* (to show more respect)
Good/fine – *Chawama*
Well done – *Mwabombeni*

Dress for the trainer

Smart casual dress is acceptable for trainers, but a jacket or suit would be expected when working with government officials or senior staff. Shorts should not be worn. If making a trip outside the training venue, more casual dress is often acceptable. Women are sometimes expected to wear a *chitenge*, which wraps around from the waist or chest. A local contact would give more details.

Working week and holidays

Office hours are Monday to Friday, from 8.00 a.m. to 5.00 p.m., with an hour for lunch. Some offices work on Saturday morning as well. Training courses usually start between 8.00 and 9.00 a.m., and end between 4.30 and 5.00 p.m. Include lunch from 1.00 to 2.00 p.m., and breaks in the morning (about 30 minutes), and in the afternoon if finishing later than 4.00 p.m.

Key dates to avoid include:

1 January – New Year's Day
8 March – Women's Day
13 March – Youth Day
1 May – Labour Day
25 May – Africa Freedom Day
3 July – Heroes' Day
July – Unity Day (usually first Tuesday)
August – Farmers' Day (usually first Monday)
18 October – National Prayer Day
24 October – Independence Day
25/26 December – Christmas holidays
If one of these dates falls on a Sunday, the Monday will become the public holiday.

Dates vary:

Good Friday, Easter Sunday, and Easter Monday – usually during March or April.

Culture and time

Zambia is predominantly Christian but accepts all religions. Participants may like to start, and possibly end, the training with a short prayer, led by one of the group. A trainer would not normally be expected to lead it.

Zambians are increasingly becoming time conscious especially in cities. Most meetings start as scheduled.

Building rapport

Trainers are respected in Zambia. People who have been educated are considered experts and will be listened to. Give details of your experience but it is sometimes best not to add too much about your academic background. For example, if you have a doctorate. Otherwise participants will think you know everything, and may be disappointed if you do not. Talking too much about qualifications can also make some participants feel that theirs are not good enough. This may affect their confidence and their ability to learn. Be sensitive to the Zambian culture and ask questions about it. Allow time for participants to share their own ideas.

Conversation topics

Ask about the person's family, but do not ask specifically about a spouse until you know the person well. You might also want to wait until you know someone before asking detailed questions about their job. Let people talk and give you information. Then pick up on what they say. Ask about their culture.

If you are interested in football (especially the United Kingdom Premier League). Zambia is among Africa's top football nations. You might like to research a few Zambian football stars, playing in your home country, and other southern African countries.

Avoid being drawn into Zambian political discussions, as your participants may have strong opinions.

Training tips

- Making fun of your own culture, yourself, or your family is always appreciated. Most Zambians watch British or American television programmes. Ask participants for examples of comedy programmes that they like.
- Do not make jokes openly about government officers or politicians – you will be misunderstood.
- Participants often socialize at the end of a training day Trainers may be be invited too.
- If organizing a regional or international training event, alert participants in advance to the sight-seeing opportunities in Zambia. Suggest they may like to book a few days' holiday while they are there. This can help them to concentrate on the activities rather than disappearing in the middle of the training.

Summary of key points to remember when training and working cross-culturally

> *People will forget what you said, people will forget what you did, but people will never forget how you made them feel (Maya Angelou).*

The previous 10 sections have offered suggestions for training in specific countries and cultures. The main message is not to assume that every country is the same as yours, nor to assume that all regions of a country are like each other. For example, the language spoken by participants may be different from the majority language. Find out as much as you can from any local contact before the start of the training. Ask 'what do I need to know about training in your country?'

Be open, sensitive, and respectful to all cultures. Learn as you go, keep asking questions and clarify what you need to know. The following summary, however, offers some of the key points to keep in mind wherever you are training.

Greetings/words of greeting

Spend time in greeting people. In many cultures, this is very important. Find the appropriate way of greeting for the country/culture. Find out about any restrictions in the country due to health and 'social distancing' concerns. If shaking hands, don't grip someone too hard, unless they do. Remember that in Muslim countries women will often not offer a hand to a man, or some men to a non-Muslim. It is always appreciated if you learn a few words of the participants' language. Most people will be happy that you have tried, even if you get it wrong. Be careful with eye contact when you meet someone. A little or a lot can be correct in different cultures. Observe what others do and follow their lead.

Business cards

Make sure you have enough business cards to distribute generously. In many cultures where status is considered important, show your job title on the card. If you have a telephone number for the country you are in, write it on the back of the card.

Use your right hand, or both hands together, to present your business card. In many cultures, the left hand is seen as unclean. Try to present your card so that the person receiving it can see it the right way up. Treat a card presented to you with respect and study it for a moment or two, and possibly ask a question about it. Do not discard it, or casually put it in your pocket (especially not your in back pocket), as this can show disrespect.

Course certificates

Most participants demand, or at least appreciate, a certificate at the end of the training. This can show what they have achieved, or it may just say that they have attended the course. It will be kept and used for many years after the event, so make sure the details are accurate, especially that names are spelt correctly. You may like to ask participants the name they would like written on their certificate, perhaps before the course starts. In most countries, presenting certificates with your right hand, or both hands together, is expected.

Names

Ask participants for the name they want to be called by. Write this down and ask participants to place a name card in front of them to help you remember. Try not to assume anything.

Gender and equality

Be aware of potential cultural variations. It is best to avoid activities that require physical contact, especially between genders. In general, participants from rural areas are more concerned about this than those in urban areas.

Language

Make sure you know in which language participants are most fluent. If this is not English, check how well they can speak English for the purposes of the course. Ask if you will need translators at the training event. If so, try to meet them before the course. Try using the suggested words shown in the country sections. It is best to try them out before using them in front of the group, especially for pronunciation. Most participants will really appreciate that you have made the effort, even if it is not quite right. It allows the participants to be able to teach the trainer something, which makes things more equal.

Dress for the trainer

In most countries, trainers should dress modestly. Smart casual is usually appropriate. If training with government officials or senior staff, you may need to dress more smartly. Make sure your credibility is not damaged by inappropriate dress. It is sometimes seen as disrespectful for an outsider to wear local clothing. Check what is appropriate with your local contact. For longer training events, dress smartly at least on the first day. Then you can adjust your clothing based on how others dress. Check in advance what the temperature will be, and whether there is heating or air-conditioning in the training venue.

Working week and holidays

Check local arrangements well in advance. Make sure you are not planning an event when there is a public holiday or when some people are likely to be away.

During Ramadan, Muslims fast from dawn until dusk, not eating or drinking. It is best to avoid training events then, as participants are likely to be tired during this period of fasting. It is also insensitive if non-Muslims are eating while Muslim colleagues are not.

Culture and time

Saving face and not losing face are important in most countries. Keep this in your mind as you interact during the training event, both formally and informally.

Attitudes to time and deadlines vary among cultures. Check with your local contact how important participants think it is to arrive on time. Also, consider how important it is to fit everything into a given time period: for example, whether participants value preciseness ('time is fixed') or flexibility ('there is always more time').

Building rapport

Having a good rapport with participants really helps them learn wherever you are. It is worth investing time to achieve this at the start and throughout the training. This should begin with the trainer welcoming participants personally as they arrive at the training venue. Use an introductory activity to build rapport between the trainer and the participants. Examples are shown in Chapter 10.

Be sure to link what you are doing to participants' own experiences, and build rapport by listening to and valuing their concerns. Show concern to all the participants, and talk with them individually at meal times and breaks. With short training sessions it is harder to build rapport. If this is the case, try to be there for a break or meal before your session, so you can introduce yourself to participants more informally. In high-context cultures that stress good relationships, trust is built by making a good connection personally with each participant. In low-context cultures that are task focused, working with others towards a common end will build rapport. As a trainer, try to achieve both, being sensitive to what people expect. See also Chapter 4, starting on page 61 for more ideas about building rapport.

Conversation topics

When talking with participants at breaks, or outside the training, good topics are questions about the culture, work, family, and what the other person does in their spare time; for example, following sport. Be sensitive and willing to stop or change the subject if you sense a reluctance to answer or when the conversation starts to get emotional. Look out for topics that are taboo, and ask a local contact beforehand if you are unsure what they are. It is best to avoid questions about politics, religion, or any national, ethnic, or tribal issues before you know the person well.

In cultures where the group is prioritized over the individual, participants would often not feel comfortable talking with an older or more senior person. Encourage these conversations but be aware that individuals may not be willing to express an opinion.

In some cultures, someone would think it appropriate to ask very direct questions such as 'how much do you earn?' This is often to provide an indication of your status. For other cultures this would not be acceptable. Find a more acceptable way of asking such as 'tell me about your job'. Phrases starting with 'so, tell me a little about ...', 'can you give me an example?' 'because...?' 'how does/could this work for you ...?' and 'what would you do if...?' are good ways of encouraging participants to talk with you, both formally during the training event, and informally.

Training tips

Across all cultures, people benefit from encouragement. They value a trainer who is open and does not come with fixed ideas about what will work in their country. It is good to ask your local contact, in advance of a visit, 'is there anything I need to know about training in ...?' Be ready to listen to participants' experiences, and make use of them in the training event. Remember to have fun. Laughter is a great way of breaking down barriers and encouraging learning.

Travel practicalities

If you are travelling to a new country for the first time, these tips will make sure you and your valuables stay safe and secure.

Before travelling

- Find out about visa requirements and, if needed, apply well in advance.
- Talk with a doctor/nurse or travel clinic to make sure you have up to date vaccinations and anti-malarial tablets, if advised.
- Take a mosquito net with you if sleeping in a malarial zone and one will not be provided locally.
- Make sure your organization provides adequate travel insurance. If not, arrange your own.
- Take spare passport-sized photographs with you. They can be useful for official documents.
- Keep checking the up-to-date advice for safety and security for travelling in the country from your own and other government. This is usually provided by the foreign affairs department.
- Find out as much as you can about the country you will be in and its culture(s). Research its history and people, and its current economic and political situation.

During the trip

- Be aware of the people around you. Be alert to changes and gatherings of people where there may be a danger, especially when tension is heightened, for example, by political

events or elections. Listen carefully to the advice from local colleagues.
- Avoid walking alone, especially at night. If you have to walk at night, choose a well-lit route and carry a torch.
- Avoid driving, especially at night.
- Always wear a seat belt and avoid vehicles without them as much as you can.
- Avoid showing a high-quality laptop, telephone, or camera. This can attract the attention of thieves. Buy a local SIM card and use a cheap phone. Only use anything more expensive in the privacy of your room.
- Be sensitive about the equipment you take into the training room or office, if the organization you are working with has less sophisticated devices.
- Use a safe to store your valuables, when available. Do not leave them lying around in the training venue or in your hotel room.
- Keep the door locked while you are in your hotel room.
- Have a small amount of emergency cash with you at all times, but do not carry large amounts. Split money between pockets and bags.
- In countries where tap water is not safe to drink, use boiled or bottled water, even when brushing your teeth. Try to minimize the use of plastic bottles and cups by taking a reusable bottle and cup with you.
- In countries where the electricity is likely to be cut off, use a surge protector when recharging electronic devices. This prevents an electricity surge destroying your devices.
- Ask before taking photos within the training group or outside. Encourage participants to tell you, privately, if they do not want their photograph to be taken. Some participants will want their own photograph taken alongside the trainer.
- Some cultures use their hands to eat with, while others use cutlery or chopsticks. If you are not comfortable with how you are expected to eat, it is acceptable to ask for what you would rather use.
- Buy and use hand sanitizer to keep your hands clean when you do not have access to soap and water.

For more information about travelling safely, see the 'Resources' section at the end of this book.

CHAPTER 8
Examples of cross-cultural training

These examples give a variety of real training situations, where the trainer did not consider cultural issues enough. They explain what happened and the reason for the difficulties. The examples help us to learn what to do when similar situations arise.

Keywords: cross-cultural training examples, cultural expectations, eye contact, criticism, saving face, training risk taking

Finding our way through a culture different to our own can be difficult. It is easy to get things wrong. This is often part of the process of our learning new ways of doing things. However much we prepare in advance, we all easily make mistakes. Here are some real-life examples of training cross-culturally.

Eye contact

A trainer was in a one-to-one training with a colleague from Tanzania and could see he was looking rather uncomfortable. She asked him if everything was all right. He said 'yes, of course'. She then paused and waited, and he said 'well actually … it makes me feel rather uncomfortable when you look me straight in the eye like that'. The trainer asked what people would normally do in his culture, and he said 'people generally look over the other person's shoulder'. So, she started to do this for the rest of the training. This made their conversation far easier for him and the trainer realized he became much more relaxed, as she did herself. The trainer recognized that other cultures can use eye contact to give different messages and that her own culture tends to use it more than others.

Upsetting a participant

The trainer wanted the session to be interactive and involve the participants. As she was talking, she kept asking the group questions. Few participants answered her questions, so the trainer carried on talking. She thought the participants were not taking things seriously enough. So, she starting asking different participants to answer each question. They didn't answer. Eventually she asked one young man to answer and he started to cry and rushed out of the room. Later the trainer discussed this with a colleague who told her that this was not their usual style of learning and that the participants would have found it threatening. They would have been embarrassed to express a view in front of the other participants, some of whom were in a more senior position in their organization.

A trip out - 1

Two trainers from India came to deliver a course in Europe. They were excited to be working with a European group for the first time. For the weekend in the middle of the two-week course the trainers had arranged an outing to a nearby town by the sea. They let everyone know the times and details. They arrived in plenty of time on the Saturday morning to greet everyone, and sit together on the train. Nobody arrived. They waited and waited but still nobody came. In the end the two trainers were really disappointed and went to the sea by themselves. The following week they spoke with their manager who explained that the local staff did not socialize together at the weekend, and that this was no reflection on the quality of their training. The manager who knew Indian culture well, explained to the trainers that this was a cultural difference, and invited them for a meal at his home that evening to talk about it some more.

A trip out - 2

In the middle of a two-week training event in Pakistan, the trainer was looking forward to a restful weekend. A few participants suggested that they went on a day outing to a local beauty spot. They booked the transport. No one asked the trainer, but it was assumed that he would go as well. On the first day of the second week when the trainer arrived, the group said they were disappointed he was not able to be there. He said that he had been there before with a previous group. They looked disappointed and said 'but you haven't been with us'. The trainer realized the compliment that they were paying him by inviting him and implying that he was a part of their group. It was too late for that trip, but he did go to all the other social events they organized in the second week.

Being critical

The group were practising the preparation of a budget and had completed a few activities together with the trainer. It was the last session of the day. The trainer then said 'now it's your turn' and passed round a handout with information on it that participants were supposed to complete on their own. The group were left to do this for about 20 minutes and then the trainer asked one participant to explain what she had done. She explained how she had got to the answer. The trainer pointed out that she had made lots of mistakes, and went through them one by one saying what she should have done. She stood at the front while he said all of this. She had lost face in front of her colleagues and at the end of the day she left quickly. The following day the group heard that she wasn't able to join the training for the last few days.

Risk taking

During a week-long course to train trainers, the trainer asked different small groups for a brief review of the topics covered at the end of each day. The first day someone just described what had happened session by session. The trainer thought it needed to be livelier, so at the beginning of the second day spent time suggesting ways that the group could present the review using audio-visual aids, doing interviews, or even playing a game. She brought in lots of colourful materials that the groups could use. Everyone seemed excited and keen to try out the ideas and the trainer was looking forward to the second review. But the group again just described what had happened. No one tried the new ideas. The trainer went away wondering why the group had seemed enthusiastic but had not used any of the ideas. A colleague suggested to her that it was too large a risk and that she should start with smaller steps.

Too much participation

The course had been going for three days and had been very participative. The participants had been enjoying it, and had said so. Then in the afternoon of the fourth day an invited outside speaker came, and started talking about a technical subject. There was hardly any participation and he only asked the participants one or two questions; he then dismissed the answers given and carried on talking. The two trainers wanted to interrupt but recognized this was a senior person, and it would not be polite. They began to worry and wondered what the participants would think. He talked for another two hours, longer than the planned hour. After an hour, one of the trainers got up and said they had reached the time allocated and politely suggested that participants could contact him with any questions. He accepted this but still carried on for another hour. Towards the end there were a few questions. The man was thanked by one of the trainers who said how knowledgeable he was. The visitor was shown out. The participants then went into a break, and the trainers were concerned about their reaction.

To their surprise the participants were all delighted with the speaker and found what he said was really useful for their work. The place was buzzing! The trainers did not realize that the visitor's style was normal for their participants; participatory methods were not. They had also enjoyed and learned a lot from the participatory approach, but valued having a rest and letting someone else do the work for this session.

Saving face

The organization had recently appointed a senior human resources (HR) officer who attended an external course about the 'basics of staff dismissal'. She learned all she needed to know, and more, and felt happy with the outcomes. A couple of days later, her assistant came into her office to tell her that some of her colleagues had been laughing at her, in the corridor, because she had attended such a basic course. They had been saying she could not be very good at HR if she had attended such a basic training. It meant that she had lost face by attending this training event. It was a difficult period for her, and she considered whether she should resign, although in the end because of the support from her manager she stayed. In the future, she decided, rather than going to an external training event, she would find someone who could provide her with 'confidential tutoring' outside work hours.

Is everything all right?

When training with a group mostly from Asia, one of the trainers from the European host country was explaining a new system to be introduced in regional offices. After talking for about 30 minutes, he said 'is everything all right?' Everyone smiled, and he said how pleased he was. He continued for another 15 minutes and then asked for any questions. Again, everyone smiled and a few shook their heads in agreement. Later when a colleague asked him how it had gone, he said 'wonderfully – everyone was happy and no one had any questions'.

After the participants returned home, they realized they still did not know how to operate the new system. The head of the organization heard this and called the trainer to her office, and asked why the training had gone so badly. He was surprised and he explained what had happened in the training. His manager explained that no one from that culture would make the trainer, or themselves, lose face by saying they did not understand what he had said. She suggested that the trainer might need to find other ways of testing participants' understanding. After a few weeks another training event had to be organized at great cost, with a more experienced trainer.

CHAPTER 9

Training cross-culturally: frequently asked questions

The chapter contains eight groups of frequent questions: working with participants, questions and answers, learning objectives, participatory training and learning, group work, online training, timing, and feedback. Each question addresses the practical concerns of the trainer.

Keywords: 'what if…', phones in training, answering questions, group work, giving feedback, keeping to time

The following questions represent situations that happen often in cross-cultural training. They are grouped into sections:
- Working with participants
- Questions and answers
- Learning objectives
- Participatory training and learning
- Group work
- Online training
- Timing
- Feedback

Working with participants

What if participants arrive too early?
As far as possible make sure everything is ready for the training in advance. Stop what you are doing and talk with participants as they arrive. Ask their name (write it down and try to remember it) and a little about them. If necessary, after your conversation say you need to do a few things to get ready. If you have more than one trainer make sure that one person spends time with the participants before the training begins.

What if a participant arrives after the session has started?
Acknowledge and welcome the participant as they arrive. On the first day especially, make sure they have somewhere to sit and give

them any handouts they need for the session. In the next break, go over training content that they have missed, especially if this is required for the rest of the session. In some venues, late arrivals are unavoidable because traffic and transport systems make it difficult to predict arrival timing precisely. Sometimes participants arrive late because something traumatic has happened in their life. In some cultures, arriving late is especially embarrassing for the individual concerned. Try not to blame the individual.

How do I make sure that participants arrive on time?
Make sure that you state clearly what time the sessions begin, and ask participants to be ready to start at that time. When there is a break, stress the start time for the following session. Most people observe this but start each session on time with less important material, assuming a few might miss it. See 'Setting ground rules', Chapter 4, page 65.

How do I deal with a group that want different things from the training?
Make sure that advance publicity materials show the learning objectives clearly. Potential participants can then see what is on offer, and what level of experience they should have. Also, before the course begins, try to identify individual participants' learning needs. Ask about their experience (or at least their job titles) and expectations of the training. If you find before the course that a participant has too much, or too little experience to make it worth their while attending, talk either to the event organizer or ideally to the participant themselves. Some training events become financially viable because there are a certain number of fee-paying participants. This can make the trainer's task more difficult, and the question is whether to cancel the course or carry on knowing that some will not fully benefit. Whatever has been done in advance, always make sure in the introductory session that expectations for the training are explored. This can manage what is realistic for participants to expect in the time available and help the trainer to plan the best way forward. See Chapter 3, page 26, *Training needs analysis*.

What if some participants are attending the wrong course?
Make sure you check participants' background and expectations before the course starts and, if necessary, talk with them

about it. If someone arrives and suspects the training is not appropriate or at the wrong level for them, let them know what you are intending to cover. If you both consider it really is the wrong course for them, work through the practical issues, for example, other suitable training, and what happens about the fees already paid.

Of course it may really be the wrong course. There might be a number of courses going on in the same building at the same time. If you do not know the group, it is worth checking, before you start, that they are expecting the training you are about to deliver!

What should I do if I realize that I have prepared the wrong material for the group?
Firstly, make sure that you really have got the wrong material. If the course has been advertised as you intend to run it, there will be participants there who want you to run it in the way you planned. Sometimes, it is only one or two people who are objecting. It is useful to talk with them in the break and see what they were expecting and if any compromise could be reached that would be acceptable to the group. Talk with the whole group about this as honestly as you can. Make sure there is no loss of face, and find a practical solution. For longer training events it can mean revising some of the activities in the evening before the next day, for some it can be just having a different emphasis on the planned material.

What do I do if someone refuses to take part in an activity?
Participation in any activity is always on the basis that a participant is willing. If they refuse, the trainer should talk a little more about its purpose and gently encourage participation. However, if this does not work, always respect the participant's decision. It may be that the activity is not culturally sensitive. If, for example, the activity requires people of different genders to have physical contact this may not be appropriate. Separating into male and female groups can be more acceptable. Make sure that no participant loses face in this process.

What if no one wants to take part in an activity?
Again, respect the group's decision and talk about it with them. Find a way of achieving the objective in a more acceptable

way. Often the group will come up with a solution for you. Be willing to be flexible!

What if someone becomes really upset?
This sometimes happens, and you need to be prepared for it. If there is more than one trainer, the one not leading the session may be able to talk with the person and take them out of the room. If there is only one trainer, say to the group that you are going to have a break, then talk with the person and, if they will tell you, ask what is upsetting them. Be aware that it could be caused by something or someone in the training session. Decide what to do, but be flexible and involve other people if they are available. This can be challenging when training cross-culturally and it is important to be sensitive and aware that you are not necessarily the person best placed to help because of your culture or gender. After the break, you may need to talk discreetly with the whole group, but without breaking any confidences. Make sure as far as you can that no one loses face.

What if everyone becomes upset?
This rarely happens, but if you become aware of it, talk with the group about the issue and try to find a way forward. If there is a local organizer for the training, it can be helpful to involve them in the discussion, especially if the issue involves practicalities, such as accommodation, food, or money. Sensitivity is needed and a willingness to be flexible.

What if people do not like me?
Most cross-cultural training events start with a lot of goodwill. Building trust between the trainer and participants and keeping good relationships is important. Part of this is being aware of cross-cultural issues, and being flexible enough to adjust to the cultural norms you are working with. Sometimes assumptions can be made about other people's perceptions. Check this out with a local colleague, if possible. It also worth asking participants how the training is going, and how they are finding your approach. Be open and listen to any constructive ideas for change.

How do I deal with someone who has more experience than I have?
Be confident that you have unique knowledge and experience, and also respect the knowledge that participants come with. In training with a new organization, participants are likely to know a lot more about what happens in their own situation. Encourage participants to share their experience and help you to learn. Someone can have similar technical expertise to that of the trainer. Acknowledge this and help everyone to learn from each other. Make use of people's knowledge. If dividing participants into groups, make sure that those with more knowledge about the topic are placed with those who have less knowledge. Sometimes those with language skills can help interpret for those who are less confident in English.

How do I encourage less confident participants to join in the discussion?
Everyone has a different way of learning, so do not assume everyone has to be talking to learn. 'Thinkers' will learn lots from training without saying anything. Given time and encouragement most people will join a discussion. Let people do this in their own time and avoid the temptation to 'pick on' people, especially in the early stages of the training. This can cause a loss of face from which it can be difficult to recover. The trainer's role is always to make the place of learning friendly and 'safe' for all participants. However, if you know that someone has particular experience, it is acceptable to try to bring this out to benefit the others in the group and also help build the individual's confidence. When working with a group from a variety of countries or organizations, invite everyone to contribute by saying how a particular issue is dealt with in their own situation. In some cultures, if more senior members of an organization are present, it is usual for them to answer all the questions and for more junior staff not to contribute. Accept that this happens, but find opportunities, especially in the way that groups are divided, for everyone to have opportunities to take part in discussions and express their views. This has implications for planning of training. Be aware that having senior and junior staff in the same workshop may not always be appropriate. When choosing who to start with when going around a group, try to begin with a more confident participant

first. Then quickly move on to someone who is less confident to make them feel included and to give them time to think about an answer.

How do I stop talkative participants from saying too much?
If someone will not stop talking ask them, 'could you summarize what you are saying in a sentence?' It is important not to be too direct about the issue so the participant does not lose face. If it becomes an ongoing problem, speak with them during one of the breaks. You could say that you realize they have a lot of experience, but want to give the others a chance to be more involved. If delivering training online, always be polite but tell the participant that you are going to put everyone on 'mute', because you want to move on.

What do I do if participants start using their telephones?
There can be wide cultural, age, and personality differences among participants. In some cultures, using your phone while the training is taking place is considered extremely rude. For others, it is seen as acceptable. Objectively, use of a phone in the training room is disruptive not only for the person using it, but also the trainer and other participants. You want the participants' full attention if the training is to achieve its objectives. Set ground rules for the training (see Chapter 4, page 65) and agree when phones may be used. You might agree that they will only be used during the breaks, and that they will be switched to silent and used only for emergencies. The ground rule would mean, if someone uses a phone, the other participants will object, which helps the trainer. The challenge for the trainer is to make the material so interesting that participants do not want to miss a moment of it!

What do I do if some participants start talking while I am presenting?
Walk towards those talking, stand by them and continue to present. If it goes on, ask them 'is everything all right?' and whether they have a question – indeed it may be something in the content that they do not understand or want to ask you about.

How do I prevent participants getting bored?
Notice when participants are not concentrating – watch their body language – and make an effort to involve them the session,

for example by asking them a direct question. Recognize when the groups energy level is low, often late morning, after lunch, and late afternoon. Use 'energizing' activities when you need to (see examples in Chapter 11). Make sure you are constantly reminding yourself that the content you deliver has to be relevant. If it is not, rethink why it is there.

Make sure there is lots of variety in the methodology you use. Use group work, individual tasks, case studies, games, puzzles, and short audio or video clips. Do not speak for more than around 8 to 10 minutes at a time without some interaction, and make it as entertaining as possible to keep everyone's attention. Tell stories to illustrate your important points. Even if they are bored, this will usually bring participants back to what you are saying. In many cultures, stories are an important way of communicating and holding attention. Make sure the group is moving around as part of some of the activities, rather than just sitting for a long time. Make use of the room and when you are speaking, occasionally move to a different part to present yourself. Above all, be enthusiastic about what you are teaching, and make it clear to participants why it is essential for them and their organization. For 'live' sessions with online training, follow the suggestions in Chapter 5, page 85-87.

How can I be sure that the training objectives are achieved fully?
Regularly check what is being learned by asking the group 'open' questions. Display the learning objective to the group. Find out how close they are to meeting it, and what there is still to do. This may mean you have to rearrange some of the programme.

What if the participants think the training is too easy?
It can be just an issue of whether the course is right for one or two individuals. Check if this is a general view of the group. If most participants feel it is too easy, ask them more challenging questions, and look again at the materials for later sessions to see if these can be changed. Talk with the group about how you might change and be honest about what is possible.

What if the participants think the material is too difficult?
Find out how many participants have this concern. Talk with the group to find out more. Be sure to save face at all

times (including your own). Consider adding more 'stepping stones' to break down the difficult parts into more manageable chunks. Check with the group at the end of the session/day to see if this has helped.

What if the participants think the activities are not relevant?
The trainer needs to regularly explain the reasons why each part of the training is relevant to the participants' roles and organizations. It may be that participants have not been able to make the connection, or to see what they will, in the future, need to be doing in their work that would make the topic relevant. Also, explain that some activities will be more relevant than others, for each person.

How can I motivate participants about the less engaging topics?
Not all training events are packed full of engaging material. Dull topics have to be learned too. Ask yourself, how important is it that participants learn this? Would it be adequate that they had a copy of the information to refer to when they need it? Your job might then be to make them aware of it and answer any questions. Generally, the duller the material the more important it is to put it over in a participative way. Try inventing new methods to do this and pick up ideas from other trainers. You could use a quiz with a prize for the group with the most correct answers, or ask participants to read something for five minutes, and then present what it means to the others in a small group for one minute.

What if all the learners are using their second (or third) language to learn?
Make sure, in advance, that everyone has either sufficient language skills to attend the course or has a translator working with them. Use the suggestions in Chapter 3, pages 28-30.

How do I respond to participants who resist taking part in an activity because it is 'silly'?
This is often culturally based. In relationship-based cultures (see Chapter 2) participants generally like to have fun and will usually accept any activity whether it has a serious training objective or is just for fun and to energize the group. In

information-based cultures it is more likely that a participant can ask 'what's the point of this?' and will expect it to contribute to the learning objectives in some way. It's good to use activities that both provide an objective and are fun, although this is not always easy. It is useful to get to know the participants and what they will be willing to do first, before you try any of the 'sillier' activities. It is always an option for someone not to take part in something, if they would rather not.

Questions and answers

What if no one in the group responds to a question I ask?
Make sure you ask the question in a number of different ways and, for a group with non-first language English speakers, make the question very clear. You can display the question in writing so it is better understood. This can increase understanding, and you can help further by writing any suggestions that the group give alongside the question. After you've asked the question, leave a silence, and after about 10 seconds, if there is no response say something like 'any ideas?' This sometimes encourages someone to suggest an answer. You might also ask 'is the question clear?', or 'you might need a little time to think about the question'. If you realize the question is not going to produce any suggestions, say something like 'let me tell you the answer' and say what it is. However, do not be too quick to jump in if you think the group is likely to know the answer. An alternative is to break into small groups, twos or threes, and ask them to think about the question together. This will produce a group answer, which is easier to hide behind if individuals feel a little embarrassed to suggest their idea on their own.

What if I do not understand an answer to my question?
If you haven't quite heard it (it is sometimes difficult to tune in to an accent quickly) ask the person 'could you say that again please?' If the content doesn't make sense, you can suggest 'could you say a little more please?' If you still do not understand, you might say 'I've not quite understood that, can anyone else explain' or simply 'thank you, what do others think?'

What if someone gives a wrong (even unhelpful) answer?
Generally, it is good to draw anything positive out of the suggestions you receive, and then perhaps say 'no, that's not quite right. Anyone else?' However, if an answer given is wrong, or could even be dangerous, thank the participant, but make sure you say clearly it is not right, and explain why, before you give the correct answer.

What if I do not know the answer to a question?
Do not panic! It is fine, trainers are not expected to know everything. The general approach is not to say anything that is misleading. First ask a clarifying question to make sure you understand. Then ask if anyone in the group knows the answer to the question. If not, say 'I'm not sure about this one either, but I will find out and let you know later' or by email if asked towards the end of the training. But make sure you follow it up. You must keep your credibility – which the suggested reply here does. In a more information-based culture the answer might be 'that's interesting, I'm not sure – I'll check and come back to you'. Again, make sure you do.

What if someone asks a question that seems to be making fun of me?
This is unlikely to be the case, although sometimes it can seem that way. Sometimes the sense is lost in cross-cultural communication. Generally, assume that all questions are serious. Occasionally someone can be teasing you, but this is usually good-natured and fairly obviously the case. Do not take yourself too seriously, and try to have some fun with the group. This then makes the possibility of someone making fun of you even less likely.

How do I respond when someone replies to my question with exactly the answer I want?
This is really helpful to a trainer. Make sure you highlight the answer for the rest of the group. A good way of showing you are listening to participants, and building rapport, is to refer to answers or other comments, made by participants earlier in the training, and mentioning their name.

Learning objectives

How do I know if the participants have achieved all the learning objectives?
As long as they are 'smart' objectives written with active verbs at the start, they can be assessed. You might like to go through the learning objectives at the end of the training with the group to see if any of them feel something has not been achieved. It's good to do this with a little time to spare so you can put it right before the training ends. You might also design a feedback form to ask participants if they feel each of the learning objectives has been achieved, and how. This will certainly help you plan for future training.

What if I cannot fit all the learning objectives into the time available?
Training is often a balance between everything you want to do and the time available. If you have limited time left, ask yourself which learning objectives are less important. Talk with the group about this, too, ask for their input and agree the way forward. It can be better to cover fewer topics fully, rather than giving an overview of everything. Use this experience when planning the length and timings for your next training event.

Participatory training and learning

We have had a day of 'participatory' activities and everyone is tired, what do I do?
There are times if using a participatory approach, when everyone becomes 'participated out'. It is important to recognize this and change the approach. At these times it can be good to include a session where the trainer does more. It is good to include this at the planning stage, but you cannot always predict how the activities will work with any particular group, so the trainer needs to be flexible. It can be helpful to have one or two topics prepared and ready, that you could present at any point of the training. These cannot be essential parts of the course but ones that would be good to include if there is time. Try to give these sessions your high energy and make them more fun if you can, even though you too can

be feeling tired. If you are nearing the end of the day when this tiredness comes, consider finishing the session earlier. If there are refreshments available, suggest you have a break and a drink before you start again.

Group work

How do I break participants into smaller groups?
Here are a few suggestions, but try to be inventive. Moving into groups can energize the participants.

- Decide the number you want in each group and go around everyone giving them a number. If you want five groups for example, number one to five, and then ask all the 'ones' to go together in a group, 'twos' in another and so on. Often someone will forget the number you gave them, so if you ask them to say their own number saying 1, 2, 3 along with the first three, there will be a better chance of the participants remembering it.
- Ask people to stand in a line based on something random, for example their date and month of their birth (not the year) with January at one end of the line, and then in order to December at the other end. Then divide participants in groups according to their birthday month, for example all January and February birthdays go together. Other possibilities are to form a line based on the time it took to arrive at the training venue, or years of experience.
- Another way is using a line based on distance from where participants were born to the training venue, longest distance at one end, shortest distance at the other. This can be useful if you want to divide participants into language groups, for topics where using their first language might be easier, or simply to give them a rest from speaking English.
- Prepare in advance the right number and types of playing cards and deal them out randomly. Ask all the aces, kings, queens, and jacks to form different groups based on the card they have.
- Towards the end of the training, ask participants to form a group with people they have not worked with already (or worked with less often). The groups will usually be formed easily.

How often do I intervene while small groups are working on their own?
Having told everyone what you want them to do, checked that they understand, answered any questions about the process, stated how long they've got, and divided them into groups, they are ready to start. The trainer then has to decide when to go and check up on them. It's important to remember that some of the best learning for participants is by interacting in these smaller groups. The trainer's role is to create the right environment for this to happen. If the trainer talks to the smaller groups too often, this fragile learning process can be restricted. One approach is to go around each group quickly after a few minutes and check they are clear about what you want them to do. Do not spend too much time, but answer any questions just to make sure they are going in the right direction. If they are really struggling give an example of what you want them to find. This is especially helpful if some participants are having difficulty with the language. Then leave them to start the learning process, and try not to interfere. Just watch in case anyone needs your help. Try walking slowly around every five minutes or so, rather than sitting down. Groups are more likely to ask you a question, if they need to, when you are close by. Often you can see or hear how they are progressing. If you have asked the groups to write their ideas or answers on paper, encourage a group which has not started, to do so. If you see one group has finished before the others, go and talk with them and ask them a few more challenging questions about the topic. This will help them use the time constructively. In some cultures, when the trainer talks to the group, participants feel that they just have to go through everything they have come up with. Try to avoid this and suggest after the first one or two 'let me stop you there, as I want the whole group to to benefit from hearing your points when we come back together'.

How do I get each group to feed back to the larger group without taking too much time?
The greater the number of groups you have, and the longer the time you give them will increase the amount of feedback. In some cultures, unless you say differently, the group will read

the answers. If one group seems to have covered the topics well, ask them to go first. You can then stress the need for the other groups not to repeat what has been said already. You do not have to ask every group to report, every time. A more radical solution is to find other ways of presenting. For example, you can ask participants to draw a picture of the answer, and explain what it shows. If it is a course on training trainers you might want to ask them to find an unusual way of presenting the material. This could then lead into further sessions about how to present.

How do I facilitate feedback to groups?
When other participants are listening to a group report, you can ask them if they have any questions or feedback for the group presenting. Try to encourage this to be positive. Be willing to stop this if any comment is a criticism of an individual rather than the activity. You might then want to add your own comments. Give positive comments first, then add negative ones and try to finish with a positive comment. In many cultures, the negative comments will be remembered far longer than the positive ones. So be gentle, and make the negative comments as constructive as possible.

How often should I change the groups?
This depends on the physical space available. In cultures where participants are less confident, and the training event lasts several days, it can be useful to keep participants in the same group for at least some of the first day. Changing groups can recharge the energy levels, so it is useful to do this towards the end of the day when participants are feeling tired. For a two-day or more training event, aim to try to change the groups enough times to make sure that everyone has worked with everyone else.

Online training

How does the cost of online training compare with face-to-face?
Face-to-face training is expensive, for example, the cost of travel and accommodation for trainers, renting a course venue, and printing materials. If an organization brings their own staff to a central point for the course, it would also have

to fund participants travel, accommodation and food costs, as well the trainer's fees.

Individual online training events can take only an hour or two to deliver, and a relatively short amount of time to prepare. They can be funded and presented internally to a large number of an organization's staff and stakeholders. Sometimes educational or training organizations will freely offer an event, such as a webinar, to fulfil their mission, and possibly to make contacts and attract future clients.

Longer online training events, lasting anything from a few weeks up to a year, take a lot of preparation and delivery time. It is difficult to recoup the cost from a single offering of the course. If the training events runs a number of times, however, it is more likely to recoup the costs, and occasionally even to make a modest surplus. Most non-profit organizations would want to find grant funding to cover the initial costs, and maybe try covering ongoing costs themselves, or charge a fee for those taking the course from outside their organization.

The costs of running the online training, in addition to the original investment in preparation, can include the costs of using the platform, updating the materials, and the cost of a trainer and a technical person. To reduce costs, online training courses could be completely self-contained so participants only interact with the platform, and human contact would be minimized. However, this requires enormous commitment and motivation from the participants, which without support, could result in a high drop-out rate from the training. Generally, a balance is made which has self-study materials and some direct contact with the trainer.

It would, in theory, be useful to have economies of scale so that if a large number of participants registered for an online course, it could be supported by just one trainer, and this sometimes happens. In reality though for courses of more than a week, there is a limit to how many participants one trainer could assist and for them all to feel they have received personal support.

When presenting 'live' online sessions, should you show the trainer on screen?
This is largely a matter of personal choice. Seeing the trainer as a real person on screen, however, can help participants realise

there's someone to support them and answer their questions. It can improve the quality of their learning experience.

For webinars and live online training, it is good to show the trainer speaking at least at the beginning of the session. For much of the session, there may be information to show on screen, and then the trainer could be shown in a reduced-sized screen in the corner of the main screen. Longer training events, seeing the trainer's face, reactions and body language is more important for building the ongoing relationships within the group.

How do I make sure that no online participant 'loses face'?
It is as important with online sessions, as it is with face-to-face training, that no one loses face. The trainer must make sure that no participant is embarrassed or forced into a position where it is difficult to keep their self-esteem. Sometimes individual participants can be more critical of others online than they would be in the training room.

Look out for this and set a relaxed supportive atmosphere, both in the main sessions and in any breakout sessions. Be aware on different cross-cultural backgrounds, especially if working internationally. Make sure that you monitor the 'chat' facility, and also forums and social media groups where participants contribute. Identify any posts that seem critical of others, and talk with the person concerned if necessary.

For a course running over six weeks, when should I release the materials to participants?
Release each week's material separately, on the same day each week. Encourage participants to complete each week's material by the end of the week. Clearly state that this is expected. Be clear about deadlines, especially about when you want them to upload their work. Arrange the day of any live event to be soon after the week's materials have been released, preferably between the beginning and middle of the week. Be flexible if participants do fall behind, and do all you can to help them catch up. Show how long you expect participants to spend on each section and activity, and be clear when additional links shown are optional rather than essential. This will help participants to know when they are doing more than is needed.

Online training is primarily to support learners and not overwhelm them. It is good to have some low-level tasks to perform in the week leading up to week 1. This will help people to become familiar with the platform, become used to being part of the group, and help them to look forward to the course starting. This 'week 0' might include uploading their picture and asking them to introduce themselves. You could also ask each participant to write a paragraph or two about why they want to be part of the training.

When presenting at 'live' events should the trainer stand up or sit down?
Whichever is more comfortable for you. It is good to have some variety, so try different options and ask for feedback from participants.

Timing

How do I keep within the time limit?
Make sure you use the rule when planning a training event: 'Must know, should know, could know' (see Chapter 3). Only include the 'must know' material unless you have the luxury of more time. Watch the clock, and adjust your material accordingly. Get into the habit of knowing what is vital from your planned material, and what activities could be missed out if you run out of time. If you are using translators for an event, remember your time will be reduced – plan for this.

How do I fill a spare 5 minutes until the tea or coffee break?
You have many options, but it is worth having a few ideas ready that do not take much preparation. For example:

- Use one of the energizers to fill the spare time. See Chapter 11.
- Ask each person to write down three things they have learned from this session, or the training up to now. Ask each person for one from their list. If you still have time to spare, ask for the second and third.
- Ask participants to form groups of two and think of a question they still have unanswered. Allow a minute or so and then start finding out what the questions are. Ask the group to answer the question first, if they can, and add

your comments then. If it is a large group this could take far longer than 5 minutes, so be prepared to cut it short. Ask participants to remember the questions and come back to them later.
• Finish early, and start the next session earlier. Or give an extended break.

Feedback

How do I receive feedback throughout the training?
If it is one day's training, it's good to ask at lunchtime 'how is it going?' 'Am I speaking clearly enough?' 'How useful is the content for you?' It gives you time to change things in the afternoon, if necessary.

For longer training events, you can ask a small group of different participants to give you feedback at the end of each day. This gives you helpful feedback that you can use the following day. Try to ask the group questions so that the good and not so good aspects will be fed back. For example, 'What's going well? What could be better? How well are the participants understanding my language and accent?' You could also ask these questions on paper, either for individuals or for the group as a whole. Alternatively, write out the questions on a large sheet of paper and ask participants to draw faces for their answers ☺ for 'good', ☺ for 'not sure', and ☹ or 'needs improving'.

How do I give feedback to an individual?
When giving feedback to an individual, first ask them 'what did you do well?' Then ask 'what could you have done better?' and 'what have you learned that would help when you are back in your workplace?' This will probably cover most of the issues before you have said anything yourself. Add your comments, and make sure that your negative comments are as constructive as possible, identifying practical ways to improve. End the feedback positively and make sure the individual goes away feeling good about him or herself.

When giving feedback, use words such as 'I notice …', I'm aware of …', or 'I observed that …', and describe what you have observed clearly. Be specific and stick to the facts. Do not attribute any blame or judgement. If you need something from the person, say clearly what your needs are; for example, 'I need ...' or 'this is important to me because ...'. You might want to ask more directly for something, saying, for example, 'would it be possible to ...' or 'I'd really like you to ...'. Keep checking that your understanding is correct.

How often should I give a group feedback on how they are doing?
Give positive feedback as often and regularly as you can, but make sure it is always genuine. Try to give feedback both for the group and individual participants. Encouraging participants is a great way of making their learning more effective and the whole experience more enjoyable.

When should I read the participant's feedback?
If you receive feedback forms at the end of the course, although you might be keen to read what they thought as soon as possible, emotionally you are probably not in a good state to receive any critical or constructive feedback. It is not good practice to read the feedback until all the participants have left the room. Certainly, you should never challenge participants on what they have said, although you are of course allowed to disagree with what is written. Even then, you are probably most likely to learn from the feedback, and implement any changes, if you read it a day or two after the course. Usually feedback at even the best of training events has negative comments, so do not be surprised or take it too seriously, even when someone says how wonderful you are! The main thing is to reflect on what is written, and try to make changes to improve future training events.

Toolkits

CHAPTER 10
Introductory activities

This chapter provides examples of activities that can be used at the start of a training event. These activities have been used successfully with cross-cultural training participants.

Keywords: introductory activities, icebreakers, energizers, opening activities, training games, hopes and concerns activity

Here are some introductory activities (sometimes called 'icebreakers') to use on the first day of a course. They are inclusive, require little advance preparation, and work well in cross-cultural training events. If any equipment is needed, make sure it is available for the start of the training. The aim of these activities is to help build rapport between participants and with the trainer. These activities can mostly be used with both face-to-face and online groups, apart from 'the horn game', which would difficult to replicate online.

The 'horn' game

Time: 20 minutes
In advance: Write three to four questions on a flip chart or board, for example:

- What is your name and where are you from?
- What do you do?
- What is one thing you like about … (the topic of the training event)?
- What is something we both enjoy?

Starting off in a pair, participants ask each other the questions in turn, and listen to the answers. After three minutes, they each join another participant in a new pair. Do this about three or four times, and then bring them all back together. Before you start, reassure everyone that there is no reporting back at the end of this task. Tell the participants that you will signal when it is time to change pairs. At this point, produce a bicycle horn (or whistle or bell) and make a noise. Check everyone knows the rules, and blow the horn to start.

Tips:
- After each round, blow the horn and be ready to move people on and make sure everyone has a new partner.
- If you have an odd number, join in yourself to make sure everyone has a partner.
- After three or four rounds, depending on the number of participants, it might be difficult for everyone to find a new partner. Intervene if you need to. If there are two participants that have already spoken to each other, you might want join that pair to let them ask you the questions.
- A whistle or bell would be just as good as a bicycle horn. If you can, use a fun noise-maker from the place where the training is being held.
- As a bonus, the horn is a great way of keeping time throughout the course. Make someone in the group responsible each day for blowing it when the break time is finished, and to make sure everyone is back on time. Participants will be queuing up to do this.
- Be prepared to leave the horn behind with someone, or with the organization, at the end of the course!

Remember one of your influential teachers

Time: 30 minutes

Ask the participants to think about a teacher that has had a positive or negative influence on them. Give them a few moments to think. Ask them either to share this in twos or threes, or with the whole group. Some participants may find it has been useful to acknowledge any negative feelings about their teacher at school, before starting the training.

Tips:
- This activity works well with smaller groups (about 10 or under), and/or with members of a group that already know each other.
- Teachers in specific subjects works well depending on the content; for example an English teacher if the training

is about writing proposals for funding, or for computer, finance, and other numbers-based training you could ask for a maths teacher.
- Be ready with an example of your own to share at the end.

Memories

Time: 30 minutes, or as long as you have
Divide participants into groups of about five. Ask each group to think of their memories about a certain topic which can be related to the content of the course. For example, a memory of making a decision, or when working with a difficult colleague. Tell the participants this can be any event, even something connected with their personal lives.

Give each group some coloured sticky notes or cards, and a couple of pens. Someone should write down a few key points of each memory as they are being told. This task can move around the individuals in each group to give everyone an opportunity to contribute. Allow about 10 minutes, longer if memories are still flowing freely. At the end, ask each group in turn to decide on their favourite memory and share it with the other groups.

Tips:
- This activity can also be used later in the training. You could use it to recall memories about a particular topic from the topics covered so far.
- You might like to collect the written memories by asking participants to place them on the wall for other to see throughout the training. If anyone does not want to do this, ask them to keep it themselves.

Picture it

Time: 30 minutes, or longer with a large group
Rather than asking someone to introduce themselves directly to the whole group, ask them to draw a picture which represents their life. Ask them to write their 'known-by' name in the centre, but otherwise try not to use words, only pictures. You might give suggestions about what to draw such as: how they spend their time at work and outside. They can divide the

paper into four quadrants, and do one drawing in each. Stress that artistic skill is not needed, stick people will be fine. Give them 5 to 10 minutes to draw. Then ask each participant in turn to show and describe their pictures to the group.

Tips:
- Have coloured paper and lots of coloured marker pens to help make the drawings as attractive as possible.
- Draw one yourself, either in advance or with the group, to share a little about yourself. You could give a simple example of what you want them to do by showing your own picture.
- When a participant is less confident speaking, having a drawing to hold up helps boost their confidence.
- If there is space, display the drawings around the room for the rest of the course. They can be a good conversation starter during the breaks. It is also a reminder of participants' names.
- You can use this activity at other times during training, especially when discussing sensitive issues, or when you are trying to encourage creative thinking. For example, if you are discussing a difficult relationship, a drawing might express it better than using words.
- When at least some of the participants are from the same organization, you could ask them to form small groups and illustrate their organization. This will mean the drawing is a combined effort, so make sure everyone joins in.
- As an alternative to drawing, participants might use items they have on them or around the room to illustrate their life instead; for example, keys, pen and paper, telephone, piece of clothing, photograph of family member.

Six

Time: about 20 minutes, longer with a larger group
Divide the group into pairs and ask them to ask each other these questions:

- Where were you and what was happening when you were six years old?
- Where were you and what was happening six years ago?
- Where would you like to be and what would you like to be happening six years from now?

Allow six minutes for this – three minutes for each person. Tell them when it is time to switch to the second participant. When they have finished, ask each person to introduce their partner to the rest of the group, choosing one new thing they just found out about them.

Tips:
- Display these questions clearly during the activity.
- Use a whistle, bell, or bicycle horn to signal the half-way point, for participants to change roles, and at the end.
- Ask the person being introduced whether there is anything they would like to add to what their questioner has reported back.

Hopes and concerns

Time: 20 minutes
Give everyone a pile of sticky notes to write on, and a marker pen. Ask them to write a few words on each to describe either a 'hope' or a 'concern' for the training event. You may want to use different coloured sticky notes for each of these. When they have finished, ask participants to place the sticky notes on a whiteboard or wall in two separate columns with 'hopes' and 'concerns' at the top of each. Then, ask someone to group similar ideas so they are next to each other. Everyone can gather round and look at what is there and add further suggestions. Make no judgement on what is suggested.

Tips:
- As you look at the suggestions, reassure participants about their 'concerns' or at least recognize that you are aware of how they feel. Make sure that everyone else also feels a responsibility to be aware of what others are concerned about.
- Looking at their 'hopes' is an opportunity to be realistic about what can be achieved in the time available. If an unrealistic hope is just from one or two participants, perhaps offer to discuss the issue with them at the end of the session.
- Be aware that these may release some hidden emotions. This activity can help the trainer to reduce any anxieties, and make sure that everyone can fully engage with the training.

Have a break

Time: as long as you need
Tell the group that you going to have a short break so they can move around a bit before you go into the next session.

Tips:
- State when you want everyone to return, and ask one of the group to be responsible for making sure people arrive back on time.
- Have a slide that has a picture of a tea or coffee cup, that you can display whenever you need it.
- This is useful for all training, but especially for online training if you suddenly have a technical problem to solve.
- For longer sessions online, it is good to have a break more often than in face-to-face sessions. Many people can find it difficult when there is an extended time of being sat and looking at the screen.

CHAPTER 11

Energizing activities

These activities are for use when participants are feeling tired, or have had a session that has been particularly challenging. The first five can be used with any training content. The first five can be used with any training content. The final two are just for fun!

Keywords: energizers, energizing activities, reviewing training content, learning posters, technical terms game, start of day game

These activities are useful when participants' energy levels are fading, but some of them (tableau, terminology quiz, just a minute, consolidating questions, and key learning poster) can be used as a way of delivering or reviewing the training content. Ideally these activities will have a link to the main theme of the training event. They help prepare everyone for the next session or just to have fun. Trainers can help by explaining the purpose of the energizer, simply saying 'we are going to play a game before we move into the next session'. These energizers can be used for online training sessions, with the exception of 'fives and sevens'.

Tableau

Time: 30 minutes
Divide the participants into groups of about 8–10 people. Give each group some words or a topic from the training, different ones for each group, and ask them not to share these words with other groups. Ask each group to arrange themselves into a 'tableau' or visual representation of that topic. Allow about 5–10 minutes for them to think about what they will do. When they are ready, ask them to present their tableau to the larger group and see if they can guess what it represents. If no one guesses, the group could give a few clues. Ask each group to explain their tableau. This provides a good way of revising the topic for everyone.

http://dx.doi.org/10.3362/9781788531085.011

Tips:
- A variation of this is to ask each group to think of their own idea, concept, or words related to the training, and then make a tableau and ask the others to guess what it represents.
- If possible, place each group in a separate space for their planning and practising, so that the other groups do not see it in advance.
- Make sure there is a photo of each tableau with the words to describe it displayed at the front of each group. With the participants' permission, this can be circulated to everyone.
- When using this for online training, ask individuals to present a personal tableau to represent something learned so far. Allow them to use any objects they have where they are to make it more interesting, and, say it is fine if they want to involve other people who are with them as well.

Terminology quiz

Time: as long as available

This can be used whenever there is some spare time. Simply write up some terms – one for each person and a few extra. These should be terms that you have already used during the course. Divide participants into pairs. After about five minutes ask each pair to choose a term, and give a definition. Tick off the terms as they are defined. The quiz helps to consolidate the material and clarify any misunderstanding.

Tips:
- It becomes increasingly difficult as you go around the group as there are fewer terms to choose from. Acknowledge this if participants are struggling to find a definition towards the end of the energizer.
- If the definition is not quite right, ask if anyone else has one. Gently correct any misunderstandings.
- Give positive feedback.
- If you have more time, or want to inject more fun, you could ask each pair to mime what the definition means, before resorting to words.

Just a minute

Time: 10 minutes
Write up three or four topics that you have used so far in the training. Divide participants into groups. Ask them within their group to each choose a topic and make sure everyone has a different one. Tell the participants they have to talk to the others in their group about their topic for a minute. They can look at their notes before they start for a minute or two, but not while they are speaking. Reassure them that a minute is not very long.

Tips:
- Ask someone in the group to keep the time. Make sure each group has someone with a watch with a second hand. Alternatively, the trainer can keep time and ask them all to start and finish the minute together. Make a noise to signal the end of each minute.
- You can divide participants into the same language groups if it is easier for them to do this in their first language.
- If the topics are challenging, write up a few more so they have more choice.
- This works well as a review at the beginning or end of the day.

Consolidating questions

Time: as long as available
Ask the participants to form groups of two or three. Each group then has to agree a question about a topic covered in a previous session. You can either choose the topic, or leave it to the groups to decide. Tell participants they are then going to ask this question to the larger group. Each small group in turn comes to the front to ask their question. Everyone else then tries to answer it.

Tips:
- This is a great way of consolidating the learning. Participants have to think about the topics again to generate the question, and then come up with an answer to the questions from the other groups.

- Gently correct any misunderstanding in each question or answer.
- For online training, ask participants to write their own ideas on to the shared whiteboard.
- Ask for and answer any follow-up questions that arise or, better still, ask the group to try to answer them.

Key learning poster

Time: 10 minutes
Prepare a sheet of paper with the title 'what have we learned?' and place it on the wall. Give everyone a few sticky notes and ask them to identify some important things they have learned from the sessions so far. Then write each one on a sticky note. Ask them to place the sticky notes on the flip chart or on the wall. When finished, ask everyone to gather around the paper covered with the sticky notes and look at them. The trainer can admire all the ideas that they have generated.

Tips:
- Find differently coloured sticky notes to make the poster look more attractive.
- This energizer can be especially useful at the end of a day.
- Leave the poster on the wall as a reminder of what has been learned.
- If the training lasts several days, you could add to it later.
- An added bonus is that it gives an insight into what the participants consider important. It can help the trainer make their future training more precise.
- For online training, ask participants to write their own ideas on to the shared whiteboard.

Fives and sevens

Time: 5–10 minutes
This is a numbers game that needs to be played quickly. Ask the group to stand up where they are, or if you have room, form a circle away from the training space. Explain that you are going to go around the group and ask each of them to say a number – one, two, three, and so on. However, instead of saying number five, or a multiple of five, they just clap. And instead of saying number seven, or a multiple of seven, they have to stamp their

feet. If someone forgets when it is their turn, or does the wrong action they are out of the game and have to sit down or leave the circle. It becomes more difficult, and more fun, the higher and faster the numbers go. The winner is the last person still in the game. Get the others to give them a round of applause.

Tips:
- Make sure that everyone in the group will be able to do the clapping and stamping, otherwise find an alternative, for example saying 'hippopotamus' or 'elephant' for five and seven, respectively.
- Ask people who are out of the game to keep an eye on the game and to say if someone has miscounted.
- You could also add number nine to the list to make it more likely for those left in the game to forget – for nine ask them to wave their arms in the air, or say 'giraffe'.
- Do not let the game go on too long. Encourage participants to say the numbers more and more quickly – this means some are likely to forget the 'fives and sevens' – and the game will finish more quickly.
- To make it more difficult – and reduce the participants more quickly – ask the group to count backwards from 100.
- You might like to give a small prize to the winner – ideally something that they can share with everyone.

Writing in the air

Time: 10 minutes

Gather the participants together and say you are going to name some of the words that you have used so far in the training. The participants are then going to use a part of the body to write these words in the air. Be aware of the participants' level of English and try to use words that are not too difficult to spell.

Examples of terms: strategic planning, budgets, planning, monitoring.

Parts of the body: right and left elbow, wrist, knee, nose, right and left ear, little finger, toes, and foot.

Tips:
- Make sure that the game is appropriate for the abilities of everyone in the group.

- Only use parts of the body that do not go beyond cultural boundaries of acceptability.
- Ask others in the group to think of terms to write and parts of the body.
- If using this in an online training session, ask participants to move back from the camera so you can see more of them. They will often be less inhibited in their home environment, which will create even more laughter!
- Join in yourself.

Links to more energizers are shown in *Online resources*, starting on page 215.

CHAPTER 12
Concluding activities

The concluding activities help the training event finish well. The chapter includes activities to: consolidate the learning, prepare an action plan, present certificates in a participatory way, and gather feedback.

Keywords: concluding activities, ending training, presenting certificates, using spare time, action plans, storytelling

The ending of the training event is an opportunity to consolidate the learning, ask participants what they are going to take away with them, and to receive feedback on the training. The following activities are designed to use with cross-cultural groups to end the training on a positive note. Most of these activities are suitable for face-to-face and online training, with the exception of 'postcards', which would need to be adapted for an online group.

What learning are you taking away from this training?

Time: 20 minutes
Give each participant a sheet of paper with a shield drawn on it. Divide it into five parts as shown in Figure 12.1. Ask participants to complete this for: something new, something renewed (they knew already but were reminded of), something to pass on to other people, and something to do. Tell them that shields usually contain a 'motto' – a phrase that captures something about the training – and ask them to include a few words that sums this up. Allow time for participants to complete it. Then ask each person to say something about one item that they have included. It's usually fun to ask for any mottos. Sometimes participants use a phrase that sums up the training brilliantly.

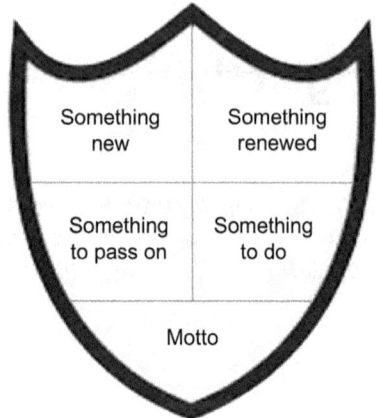

Figure 12.1 Shield

Tips:
- Have coloured paper, perhaps with the outline shield printed on, and different colour marker pens available.
- When the participants report back, listen carefully and be encouraging. Make sure the rest of the group are listening too.
- Suggest participants may like to place their shield on a wall near their desk when they return to work.
- Say that the participants can draw the item or write it in their first language. It is primarily for them to take back home as a reminder. If participants are not so confident in writing English this means they can still take part.

Learning log

Time: 20 minutes

Copy a sheet for each participant that has a row for each session down the left-hand side, and three headings along the top. These could be: 'What have I learned?', 'How will I use it in my workplace?', 'Who do I need to share it with?' Allow people time to answer these questions each day and/or at the end of the training.

Tips:
- Explain what the learning log involves at the beginning of the training. This means participants can keep updating it after each session.

- Tell them that this is just for their own use.
- Encourage participants to use this as they learn new ideas and skills throughout the training, so nothing is lost.

What next?

Time: 10–15 minutes

Go round the participants, one by one, and ask what they have gained from the training and what is their next step in developing their skills.

- Try to make sure everyone has chance to speak and listen carefully. Be encouraging.
- If there is any advice or information you can give to the group or to individuals this is a good time to do so. It might also be an opportunity to discuss any further training needs.
- If you think you may receive a better response, break the groups into pairs or threes and ask them to work on this together. This may be better if you are training in a culture where senior members are likely to be the only ones who contribute to the large group.

Postcards

Time: about 20 minutes

Find a postcard for each participant, and a few to spare. Ask them to choose one that they like, address the card to themselves, and write 'three action points' from the training that they want to achieve. Collect the postcards and say that you will send them to the participants in a few weeks.

Tips:
- If training internationally, have cards from your own country. If they have something to do with learning or the topic of the training, so much the better.
- If confidentiality is likely to be an issue, provide envelopes which can be self-addressed and ask participants to put their postcard inside and seal it.
- Find the easiest way to send the cards. For in-house courses, leave them to be posted by someone in the organization. If the postal service is reliable, you could leave them to post with another contact in the country. If this is too difficult,

you may like to scan the picture and message, and send them electronically.
- As an additional activity or if you are working with a group online, you may want to develop the action plans, as this is a key part of implementing the training. One way is to ask participants to draw three triangles with one 'action' at the top of each. Underneath ask them to put more details. For examples, who will be involved? when will it be completed? and how will it be achieved? This is for participants own use only, although you could ask if they would like to share something from it with the other participants.

One more question?

Time: minimum 10 minutes
Ask participants to form groups of two or three, and decide one question (or more) from the training topics covered, to which they still want to find the answer. Allow no more than a couple of minutes for this. Go round each group and ask for just one of their questions. See if someone from one of the other groups can answer it first or, if not, offer your own solution. Some responses may not be possible, other than to say we need to run a whole training course on this topic! Ask each group for at least their first questions and if you have time go to the second and third questions.

Tips:
- Be realistic about what is possible.
- You may need to offer to send some information about the topic, if there is just too much to say in a few minutes.
- If this is towards the end of the training event, time may be running out, but say you are happy to talk with participants individually about this after you have formally finished the training.

Storytelling

Time: 20 minutes for up to 15 participants
Find some space, outside if possible, and ask the group to form a circle. Have something soft (either a ball or a cushion work well) available. Tell the group that you have heard that their

culture(s) is very good at telling stories. Say that you are going to tell the story of your time together. You will start the story and then throw the ball to someone else in the circle, who continues the story. They then throw the ball to each person in turn, who will add a bit more to the story. The story should include activities and discussions during the training event. If you have displayed paper sheets from training activities around the room, this might remind them. Say that if you are unable to think of anything, you can throw the ball to someone else and have it back later. Tell the group that everyone must be included. When ready, start by saying 'Once upon a time, a director of the ... organization visited ...' and then throw the ball to someone. At the end, when everyone has contributed, the ball goes back to the trainer. Then add a sentence or two, and say 'they all went back home and lived happily ever after'.

Tips:
- This activity works well in all cultures. Especially with verbally based, rather than information-based cultures, for example high-context cultures.
- Make sure no one is left out, even if it is a very short contribution.
- 'Storytelling' works well as a final activity to let people say something about the training and what they will take away with them.

Presenting certificates

Time: 15–20 minutes

A participatory way of presenting the certificate is to give everyone someone else's certificate. It is placed face down in front of them. Stress that they must not touch, or look at it, until you say so. When you are ready, pick someone to start the process. They do not say anything but go to the person named on the certificate and present it to them. Encourage everyone else to applaud and you can take some photographs (ask permission first) for circulation later.

Tips:
- If you have noticed that a participant has formed a special bond with someone else, you may like to give their certificate to that person to present.

- You might suggest that participants (especially if they have been together for several days or more) say something positive that they have appreciated about the person as they present the certificate.
- If using this for online training, the physical certificate may not be available until later, unless you can send a copy electronically for participants to print themselves. None the less, it would be good to go round the group and ask what they appreciated about each other.

One word

Time: a few minutes

This is a quick way of pulling people together at the end of the training and celebrating what you have achieved. Ask everyone to think of one word that describes how they have felt about the training. Tell them not to say the word immediately. Participants then form a circle. The trainer counts one, two, three – then everyone shouts their word as they jump and wave their arms in the air. If anyone is not able to jump, ask everyone just to shout their word. People then say goodbye and leave.

APPENDIX 1

Self-assessment of high-context and low-context culture

This self-assessment helps you to estimate where you are on the spectrum of high-context and low-context cultures (See Chapter 2). The concepts were originally developed by anthropologist, Edward T. Hall. They can help to explain why communicating across cultures is not always easy. Remember neither type of culture is better than the other, only different.

Look through each of the statements and decide how much you agree with them. Then put the ranking number 1, 2, 3, 4 or 5 in the column headed *your ranking*. Be as honest as you can as this is for your own use only. If you do not have experience of the particular situation, choose the ranking that is closest to how you think you would respond if you were in that situation. Try not to think too much about the statement, just give your first response.

Table A.1

Statement	Ranking options	Your ranking
1 = You strongly agree; 2 = You generally agree; 3 = You are not sure; 4 = You generally disagree; 5 = You strongly disagree		
If I am chairing a meeting, I start working through the agenda as soon as everyone has arrived or as soon as the agreed start time of the meeting has been reached	1 2 3 4 5	
I like to be direct when talking with people	1 2 3 4 5	
When giving people information about a topic, I show it to them in writing as well as speaking about it	1 2 3 4 5	
If I have a deadline, I will deliver what is needed by the day and time agreed	1 2 3 4 5	
I don't regularly say 'yes' or nothing at all, when I mean 'no'	1 2 3 4 5	
I contact people by email or text rather than speaking on the telephone	1 2 3 4 5	

(Continues)

Table A.1 (*Continued*)

Statement	Ranking options	Your ranking
I prefer it when things go according to a pre-arranged plan	1 2 3 4 5	
I would not be happy to discuss my age, relationships, or my salary with people I have only recently met	1 2 3 4 5	
I am unhappy when I arrive late for an appointment	1 2 3 4 5	
I prefer to learn on my own rather than in a group	1 2 3 4 5	
I like to see information written down rather than having to talk with someone to find out	1 2 3 4 5	
Many of my friends are from the places I have worked	1 2 3 4 5	
I can work with someone very effectively, even if I do not know them well.	1 2 3 4 5	
If my colleagues have done something wrong, I do not find it difficult to tell them	1 2 3 4 5	
I do not like to stand too close to people with whom I am talking	1 2 3 4 5	
When asking a colleague to do something, I make the meaning clear in what I say	1 2 3 4 5	
When I make a decision, I only use factual evidence	1 2 3 4 5	
I prefer to keep to my schedule even if I upset someone	1 2 3 4 5	
If I had to choose, I would prefer someone to do something quickly even if it was not completely accurate	1 2 3 4 5	
I like my time to be highly organized	1 2 3 4 5	
YOUR TOTAL RANKING SCORE:		

What the rankings suggest and how to develop your cultural skills in training

After ranking the statements, add up your total ranking score. This is not a scientific test, but an indication of whether you operate with a more high- or low-context style. There is no right or wrong answer, but knowing where you are on the spectrum is the starting point for increasing your cultural awareness in training design and delivery.

If your ranking score is:

Up to 45
You tend towards a low-context culture. You are likely to be someone who likes to get tasks done efficiently and by a set deadline, which is really important when delivering training. You may need to work on developing working relationships within a training group. When working with participants who are also low-context you may be able to be concise in your approach. With high-context participants, however, try give more detailed explanations than you are used to.

Between 46 and 74
You tend towards showing elements of both low and high-context culture and you can be adaptable to different situations. This can be helpful in delivering training to connect with participants across their cultural preferences. When training with groups that you consider to have strongly low- or high-context, check your materials and activities carefully to make sure they make the points clearly, but give sufficient background information as well.

Over 75
You tend towards a high-context culture. You are likely to value relationships with others highly which is really important when delivering training. You may need to work on recognising that others are not always like this. When working with participants who are mostly from high-context cultures, give more detailed information in training activities but be careful still to clearly state what needs to be done. When debriefing, pull out the key learning points and summarise these, ideally in writing. This will help participants from a low-context culture.

After completing the assessment, you may also want to ask a trusted colleague who is more experienced in cross-cultural communication to give you their insights, in confidence.

APPENDIX 2

Action verbs for writing learning objectives

Table A.2 Action verbs for writing learning objectives

Remember	Comprehend	Apply	Analyze	Evaluate	Create
Recall learned information	*Demonstrate an understanding of information and ideas*	*Use knowledge in actual situations and to solve problems*	*Break down information and ideas and draw connections*	*Examine and defend judgements and ideas based on the available evidence*	*Prepare new and alternative approaches*
Define	Associate	Adapt	Appraise	Appraise	Assemble
Duplicate	Categorize	Articulate	Attribute	Argue	Collaborate
Find	Classify	Build	Calculate	Assess	Combine
Group	Compare	Choose	Categorize	Criticize	Compose
List	Contrast	Construct	Determine	Critique	Construct
Locate	Describe	Demonstrate	Differentiate	Debate	Design
Memorize	Discuss	Examine	Distinguish	Defend	Develop
Name	Explain	Illustrate	Divide	Detect	Devise
Outline	Express	Implement	Estimate	Grade	Formulate
Quote	Gather	Integrate	Interpret	Justify	Generate
Recognize	Group	Modify	Investigate	Measure	Invent
Record	Identify	Prepare	Mind-map	Moderate	Lead
Repeat	Match	Present	Organize	Persuade	Manage
Reproduce	Paraphrase	Produce	Question	Predict	Negotiate
Retrieve	Relate	Re-enact	Relate	Review	Plan
Select	Report	Schedule	Score	Select	Programme
State	Summarize	Use	Structure	Validate	Revise
Tabulate	Translate	Write	Test	Weigh	Simulate

Source: based on the ideas of B. S. Bloom et al., 1965

References and resources

References

Bloom B.S. et al. (1965) *Taxonomy of Educational Objectives: The Classification of Educational Goals. Handbook 1: Cognitive domain.* London: Longman Higher Education.

Cammack, J. (2012) *Communicating Financial Management with Non-finance People: A Manual for International Development Workers*, Rugby, UK: Practical Action Publishing.

Cammack, J. (2014) *Building Financial Management Capacity for NGOs and Community Organisations*, Rugby, UK: Practical Action Publishing.

Collins, J. (1998) *Perfect Presentations*, London: Marshall Publishing.

Hall, E.T. (1989) *Beyond Culture*, New York: Anchor Books.

McCarthy, P. (2016) *Cultural Chemistry: Simple Strategies for Bridging Cultural Gaps* [online] <www.culturalchemistry.co.uk/book> [accessed 12 November 2019].

Munter, M. (1993) 'Cross-cultural communication for managers', *Business Horizons*, May-June: 69–78.

Pretty, J.N., Guijt, I., Thompson, J., and Scoones, I. (1995) *Participatory Learning and Action: A Trainer's Guide*, London: International Institute of Environment and Development.

Trompenaars, F. and Hampden-Turner, C. (2012) *Riding the Waves of Culture*, London: Nicholas Brealey Publishing.

Worldometers.info (22 July 2020) Dover, Delaware, USA. For population and land area figures in chapter 7.

Published resources

Barker, A. (2019) *Improve Your Communication Skills: How to Build Trust, Be Heard and Communicate with Confidence,* London: Kogan Page.

Barty, A. and Lago, C. (2003) *Working with International Students: A Cross-cultural Training Manual*, London: UKCOSA: The Council for International Education.

Cammack, J. (2012) *Communicating Financial Management with Non-finance People: A Manual for International Development Workers*, Rugby, UK: Practical Action Publishing.

Cammack, J. (2014) *Basic Accounting for Community Organizations and Small Groups: A Practical Guide* (with training plans and notes for trainers), Rugby, UK: Practical Action Publishing.

Chambers, R. (2002) *Participatory Workshops: A Sourcebook of 21 Ideas and Activities*, London: Earthscan.
Collins, J. (1998) *Perfect Presentations*, London: Marshall Publishing.
Cutts, M. (2013) *Oxford Guide to Plain English*, Oxford, UK: Oxford University Press.
Dresser, N. (2005) *Multicultural Manners: Essential rules of Etiquette for the 21st Century*, Hoboken, NJ: John Wiley & Sons.
Guirdham, M. (2005) *Communicating Across Cultures at Work*, Basingstoke, UK: Palgrave Macmillan.
Hogan, C. (2002) *Understanding Facilitation: Theory and Principles*, London: Kogan Page.
Hogan, C. (2003) *Practical Facilitation: A Toolkit of Techniques*, London: Kogan Page.
Hope, A. and Timmel, S. (1984) *Training for Transformation, Books 1–3*, Rugby, UK: Practical Action Publishing.
Hope, A. and Timmel, S. (1999) *Training for Transformation, Book 4*, Rugby, UK: Practical Action Publishing.
Lead International (2004) *Training across Cultures: A Handbook for Trainers and Facilitators Working around the World*, London: Lead International.
Maranz, D. (2001) *African Friends and Money Matters*, Dallas, TX: SIL International and the International Museum of Cultures.
McCarthy, P. (2016) *Cultural Chemistry: Simple Strategies for Bridging Cultural Gaps* [online] <www.culturalchemistry.co.uk/book>.
Molinsky, A. (2013) *Global Dexterity*, Boston, MA: Harvard Business School Publishing.
Morrison, T. and Conaway, W.A. (2006) *Kiss, Bow or Shake Hands*, Avon, MA: Adams Media.
Oxfam GB for Emergency Capacity Building Project (2017) *Building Trust in Diverse Teams: The Toolkit for Emergency Response*, Oxford, UK: Oxfam GB.
Participatory Research in Asia (PRIA) (1998) *A Manual of Participatory Training Methodology in Development*, New Delhi: PRIA.
Peterson, B. (2004) *Cultural Intelligence*, Boston, MA: Nicholas Brealey Publishing.
Pretty, J.N., Guijt, I., Thompson, J., and Scoones, I. (1995) *Participatory Learning and Action: A Trainer's Guide*, London: International Institute of Environment and Development.
Ridge, G. (2010) *Training Skills*, London: Directory of Social Change.
Seifert, L. and Stacey, M. (1998) *Troubleshooting for Trainers: Getting it Right when Things Go Wrong*, Aldershot, UK: Gower Publishing.
Storti, C. (2000) *Figuring Foreigners Out: A Practical Guide*, Boston, MA: Nicholas Brealey Publishing.

Storti, C. (2007) *The Art of Crossing Cultures*, Boston, MA: Nicholas Brealey Publishing.

Trompenaars, F. and Hampden-Turner, C. (2012) *Riding the Waves of Culture*, London: Nicholas Brealey Publishing.

Online resources

www.africanbookscollective.com
Books from African writers and publishers, including about Ghanaian, Kenyan, Nigerian, and Ugandan cultures.

www.civicus.org/index.php/media-center/resources/toolkits
Civicus 'toolkits' on communication and other topics

www.comminit.com
Advice on communication

www.commisceo-global.com/resources/country-guides
Free country guides about language, culture, customs, and etiquette

www.culturesmartbooks.co.uk/destinations.php (or online publishers)
Culture Smart series of books – an overview of the culture in a range of countries

www.futurelearn.com
Free online short courses from leading international universities, giving examples of an online layout.

www.geerthofstede.com/culture-geert-hofstede-gert-jan-hofstede/6d-model-of-national-culture/ Geert Hofstede's 'six dimensions' model

www.geerthofstede.nl
More information about Geert Hofstede's work

www.healthytravelblog.com
Tips on keeping healthy when you are travelling

www.hofstede-insights.com
Geert Hofstede – a celebrated anthropologist. His website contains information about many countries using his 'six dimensions' of culture

www.international.gc.ca/cil-cai/country_insights-apercus_pays/ci-ic_ca.aspx?lang=eng
Global Affairs, Canada – cultural information about a wide range of countries

www.johncammack.net (click on 'research' and 'resources')
Summary of research into financial communication and cross-cultural issues

www.justlanded.com
Practical and cultural guides to a variety of countries

www.learning-styles-online.com
Learning Styles Online – a list of different learning styles and how each learns best

www.librarything.com/series/Culture+Shock! (or online publishers)
Culture Shock series of books – a detailed guide for visitors, and longer-term residents, in a range of countries

www.maiden-voyage.com
Maiden Voyage – making business travel safe for women

www.mindtools.com (click on 'communication skills' and 'learning skills')
Mind tools – training resources, including resources on mind-mapping

www.nnchallenge.org.uk/home/index.html
National Numeracy Challenge – an online way of seeing how numerate you are, and finding ways to improve

www.omniglot.com
Phrases – written and spoken, in many languages

www.open.edu/openlearn/free-courses www.omniglot.com
The Open University free online courses, with examples of online presentation

www.plainenglish.co.uk
Good practice in writing plain English

www.practicalactionpublishing.com
Practical Action Publishing's Critical Development Series and also country profiles of Cambodia, Ethiopia, Ghana, India and Pakistan

www.sessionlab.com/blog/online-energizers
20 online energizers for virtual teams and remote meetings

www.sessionlab.com/blog/train-the-trainer
Train the Trainer Course – A Complete Design Guide

www.softwareadvice.com/uk/lms/online-course-platform-comparison/
Comparison of Online course platforms for e-learning

www.trainingzone.co.uk
Tips on a range of training topics

www.webconferencing-test.com
A review of online meeting software

www.youtube.com/watch?v=GhA9eypocE0
Julien S. Bourrelle - *Ted Talk:* 'Learn a new culture'

www.youtube.com/watch?v=l-Yy6poJ2zs
Julien S. Bourrelle – *Ted Talk:* 'How culture drives behaviours'

End note

Having read this book, you are on the journey of cross-cultural training. You may be well into the journey, or just beginning. 'The wise woman' (below; source unknown) presents an ideal that you may want to move towards, even if it may take time to achieve. The secret is just to keep going day by day, course by course.

The wise woman
Someone who wanted to be a trainer, went to see a wise woman to ask her what training and learning was all about. She told him: it is to recognise what has inspired you and what you have learnt in your life. Then to share it with others, wherever they are around the world, and help them to integrate it into their life in a way they can understand.

'But how can I do this', the trainer asked.

She said: 'you can do this if you are observant, and see what needs to be done. You need to be both ordinary and unique, to see things as no one else sees them. Present this knowledge, with confidence, and in an inspiring way as you can. Present it logically, always wanting the best for your learners. Help them, while being willing to learn from them'.

She added: 'be humble, know the limits to your own knowledge, and learn from everyone that you meet. Never underestimate the effect of passing on learning to others – it can transform lives, organizations and communities. And, without knowing it, you can change someone's whole approach, in a way they will never forget, even if they are never able to tell you'.

Index

A indicates text in an appendix, B text in a box, F text in a figure and T text in a table

Bangladesh, training in 104–108
Blended learning: *see online learning*
Business cards 154

Cambodia, training in 108–113
Case studies 42, 67–68
Challenges of cross-cultural training 1–8
Concluding activities 201–206
Conversation topics 157
Course certificates 154–155, 205–206
Cross-cultural training, examples of 161–165
Cultural impact on training 9–22
  answering all questions with a 'yes' 165
  dos and don'ts 20–21
  high- and low-context types 10–14
  high- and low-context, self-assessment 207–209A
  online training 80, 86–87
  organizational and professional 12–14
  seven dimensions types 14–19
  time 156

Diversity and inclusiveness 28, 51
Drama 66–67

Energizing activities 195–200
English as a second language 28–30
  online training 84–85
Ethiopia, training in 113–118
Evaluating training 56–58
Expectations 30, 45–46, 168–169
  use of 55–56
Eye contact 62, 78, 154, 161

Facilitation 23, 24B
Feedback 177, 179–180, 184–185, 205
Financial training 91–102
  deciding what is needed 92, 93B
  international document names and terms 98–101
  non-literate groups 100–101
  numbers and scripts 98–101
  participatory training 96
  tips 101–102
  types of training and who to train 93–96
  who trains 92–93
Forums: *see online training*
Further learning 58–60, 90

Games 65–66, 189–190
Gender and equality 65, 155
Ghana, training in 119–123
Glossary xv–xviii
Greetings 150, 154
Ground rules 65
Group work 82, 178–180

Handouts 50
'Hands-on' learning 39–42, 82

India, training in 123–129
Instruction giving across cultures 43B
Introductory activities 189–194

Jordan, training in 129–133

Kenya, training in 133–138

Learning objectives 26–27, 30–32, 168, 173, 177, 211A
Learning preferences 7B, 8
Losing face: *see saving face*
'Live' events: *see online training*

Mind mapping 36–37

Names 155
  definitions of parts of name xv–xvi
  remembering 63–64

Online training 71–90, 180–183
  advantages and disadvantages 72–73
  audio and video clips 81–82
  blended learning 73–74, 80–81, 86
  break-out groups 82
  challenges 8
  cultural implications 80–88
  forums 81
  'live' events 74, 75–77, 85–87, 181–183
  platform
    definition xvii
    tools 84
  practicalities 74–79
  releasing materials to participants 182–183
  starting an event 88

Pakistan, training in 138–143
Participatory training 24–26, 25B, 82F, 177–178

finance training 96
online training 80–84
too much 164
Participants
  arriving 87, 167–168
  less confident and threatened 97, 171–172
  losing interest 172–173
  motivating 174
  not taking part 169–170
  talking too much 172
  upset 162
Phones 172
Presentations
  dos and don'ts 49B
  preparing 38–39

Questions and answers 3, 51–52, 175–176
  dos and don'ts 53B, 54B
  no-one responds 175
  open and closed questions xv, xvii, 43B, 51,
  senior staff answer 3
  trainer not knowing the answer 52, 176
Quizzes and worksheets 68

Rapport and trust, building 2, 61–63, 97, 156–157
Resources 213–217
'Road map' 46, 47F

Saving face (and losing face) 19–20, 52, 163, 164–165, 182
Seating arrangements 69
Starting practicalities 44–45, 74–78, 88
Storytelling 66, 204–205

Timing 18–19, 38, 68–69, 183–184
Training
  arrival activities 43–44
  before the training 26–36

cultural models and
 implications 9–22
delivering 42–54
designing and planning
 36–42
endings 52–53, 201–206
hopes and concerns 5,
 46, 193
mind mapping 36–37
monitoring and evaluation
 54–60, 89–90
needs analysis (TNA)
 26–27, 92
plans 30–32, 39, 40–41T, 85
relevancy 6
structure 34
supplies 34, 35–36B
timing of each session 38
worries about 5–6
what to wear 155–156
Training and facilitating 23, 24B
Travel practicalities 158–159

United Kingdom, training in
 143–149

Visual aids 48–50

Welcome message and poster
 32–33, 45F
Welcome poster 45F
Words in specific languages
 104–154
Working weeks and holidays 156

Zambia, training in 149–153

www.ingramcontent.com/pod-product-compliance
Lightning Source LLC
Chambersburg PA
CBHW070921030426
42336CB00014BA/2479